180 Prayers to

Change
the
World

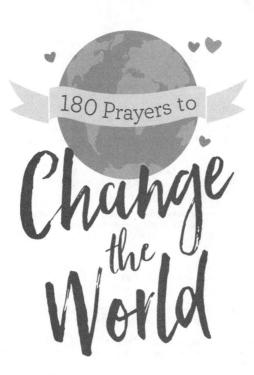

180 Prayers to Change the World

JANICE THOMPSON

BARBOUR BOOKS
An Imprint of Barbour Publishing, Inc.

Scripture quotations marked NIV are taken from the HOLY BIBLE, NEW INTERNATIONAL VERSION®. NIV®. Copyright © 1973, 1978, 1984, 2011 by Biblica, Inc.™ Used by permission. All rights reserved worldwide.

Scripture quotations marked NLT are taken from the *Holy Bible*. New Living Translation copyright© 1996, 2004, 2015 by Tyndale House Foundation. Used by permission of Tyndale House Publishers, Inc. Carol Stream, Illinois 60188. All rights reserved.

Scripture quotations marked NASB are taken from the New American Standard Bible, © 1960, 1962, 1963, 1968, 1971, 1972, 1973, 1975, 1977, 1995 by The Lockman Foundation. Used by permission.

Scripture quotations marked CEV are from the Contemporary English Version, Copyright © 1995 by American Bible Society. Used by permission.

Scripture quotations marked ESV are from The Holy Bible, English Standard Version®, copyright © 2001 by Crossway Bibles, a publishing ministry of Good News Publishers. Used by permission. All rights reserved.

Scripture quotations marked NCV are taken from the New Century Version of the Bible, copyright © 2005 by Thomas Nelson, Inc. Used by permission. All rights reserved.

Published by Barbour Books, an imprint of Barbour Publishing, Inc., 1810 Barbour Drive, Uhrichsville, Ohio 44683, www.barbourbooks.com

Our mission is to inspire the world with the life-changing message of the Bible.

Member of the
Evangelical Christian
Publishers Association

Printed in the United States of America.

You Can Make a Difference

Stop and think about these words for a moment: *you can make a difference*. No matter where you come from, where you live, or what sort of work you do, God can use you to make a difference for eternity. You can affect change—in the lives of those around you right now and for generations to come. God wants to use you to grow His kingdom. He placed within you the power to be a world changer, and that's just what you are. Begin to see yourself as such as you use this handy book to pray. Each day's offering will provide a pertinent topic, a scripture, a prayer, and an idea you can use to impact lives. Nothing can hold you back when you offer your life in service to the King of kings!

Light Makes a Difference

You used to be like people living in the dark, but now you are people of the light because you belong to the Lord. So act like people of the light and make your light shine. Be good and honest and truthful, as you try to please the Lord.
EPHESIANS 5:8–10 CEV

Lord, sometimes this world feels very dark. I wonder if I'm making any difference at all. I want to shine brightly for You, but there are days, I confess, when I feel surrounded by murky shadows intent on bringing me down. They hover over me in threatening fashion, and sometimes I feel like giving in. That's why I'm so grateful for this reminder in Your Word that I belong to You, that it's really *Your* light I'm shining. I can rest easy knowing You're the One doing the work. I'm just the vessel. As I step out into this great big world, give me creative ideas so that I can shine in a way that draws others to You. I praise You for the joy of making a change, Lord. Amen.

BE THE CHANGE
Take flowers to nursing home residents, or make floral wreaths to hang on the doors of their rooms.

In the Same Way

*"In the same way, let your light shine before others,
so that they may see your good works and give
glory to your Father who is in heaven."*
MATTHEW 5:16 ESV

Lord, I know the only chance I have of making a real difference in this world is to follow the example of Your Son, Jesus. He gave sacrificially and approached people in practical ways. He met needs in both a tangible and spiritual way. Best of all, He took the time to get to know others and to assess their needs before He offered a remedy. That way, they truly felt cared for. Today, please point me in the direction of someone I can impact—someone who needs a little light. I pray that I may step out of my comfort zone and be the hands and feet of Jesus to that person. Amen.

BE THE CHANGE
*Offer to clean out someone's garage or storage unit.
Give in a sacrificial way, as Jesus did.*

Following after Jesus

*Again Jesus spoke to them, saying, "I am the
light of the world. Whoever follows me will not
walk in darkness, but will have the light of life."*
JOHN 8:12 ESV

I've been reading Bible stories about those whose lives
You changed—Abraham, Moses, David, Rahab, Jonah,
and so many more. You used each one—even those
who weren't willing at first—to completely change the
course of history. They impacted lives wherever they
went. I see the potential in my own journey to effect
change in the lives of others as well. As I follow hard
after You, give me Your eyes to see those who are in
need. Give me Your ears to hear the cries of the ones I
can minister to. I want to shine brightly, Lord, but not
in my own strength. May I never forget—You're the
leader, Jesus. I'm the follower. Amen.

BE THE CHANGE
*Work a shift at a local soup kitchen. Volunteer for any position
available—cooking, doing dishes, or even mopping floors.*

Paying It Forward

*God looked at the light and saw that it was
good. He separated light from darkness.*
GENESIS 1:4 CEV

One of the things I love most about You, Lord, is that
You always pay it forward. You bless me abundantly
and, in doing so, teach me lessons about how I can
bless others. Then I step out and bless others, knowing
they will pass on blessings in turn. I love this cycle. It's
the gift that keeps on giving! Show me how to pay it
forward in my everyday life—in little ways and in big
ones too. I want to live an adventurous lifestyle filled
with opportunities to share Your light as I go along.
Lord, it is so exciting to be a blessing! I'm grateful to
be used by You. Amen.

BE THE CHANGE

*Do a good deed for someone who can pay it forward.
Example: pay for the order of the customer in the car
behind you at your local drive-through.*

Practical Giving

Light in a messenger's eyes brings joy to the heart,
and good news gives health to the bones.
PROVERBS 15:30 NIV

So many times, I feel like I have little to give, Lord. I think that because my bank account is low on funds, I can't bless others. Sometimes I even get a little blue thinking about this. I want to do big things! But You're not limited by money, are You, Lord? There are hundreds of ways I can impact the lives of those around me without spending a penny. I can send encouraging notes, mow someone's lawn, or bless an elderly neighbor with the gift of a visit. Today, please show me some creative, inexpensive ways I can reach out to my neighbors, my friends, elderly loved ones, and those in need. I can't wait to make my list! Amen.

BE THE CHANGE
Offer to clean out the rain gutters for your
elderly neighbor or for a single mom.

A City on a Hill

*"You are the light of the world. A town
built on a hill cannot be hidden."*
MATTHEW 5:14 NIV

Lord, one of the hardest things about being a Christian is this whole "shining bright" thing. I don't want to draw attention to myself. That's why, instead of shining like a city on a hill, I often dampen my light. But You, Father, are great at redirecting attention and pointing it where it belongs—on You. You didn't create me to hide my light. There are people who need glimpses of Your love, and You long for me to shine brightly so that I can draw them to You. So, here I go, Lord! No more hiding for me. Amen.

BE THE CHANGE
*Host a sandwich-making party and give the
food to the homeless. They will appreciate it,
and you'll have fun with the prep work.*

Lighting the House

"No one lights a lamp and then puts it under a basket. Instead, a lamp is placed on a stand, where it gives light to everyone in the house."
MATTHEW 5:15 NLT

This scripture is so interesting to me, Lord. Even back in Bible times, people knew that elevating a light source would broaden its reach. Today, most of our lights are affixed to our ceilings. With the flip of a switch, rooms flood with light because the light beams radiate from above, spreading out over everything below. That's how I want to be, Father—like an effective light that draws people to You rather than hiding away under a basket or bushel. May my every deed, every action, flood lives with heavenly beams of Your light so that all might come to know You. Amen.

BE THE CHANGE
Rake a neighbor's leaves.

Not Overcome

The light shines in the darkness,
and the darkness has not overcome it.
JOHN 1:5 NIV

The needs out there are great, Lord. Many people are homeless and hopeless. Others are struggling from paycheck to paycheck, wondering if they'll ever get ahead. Things can seem dark and gloomy when you're stuck in a rut. But I want to make a difference in the lives of those who are going through tough stuff. I don't want to leave people feeling overwhelmed by their situations when I could be spreading Your light through kind deeds or words. With Your help, I want to come up with fun ideas to lift spirits and spread joy. Thanks for the reminder that I can brighten the lives of people who feel like giving up. Amen.

BE THE CHANGE
Offer to give free music, art, or writing
lessons to underprivileged children.

Ears to Hear

"Then the righteous will shine like the sun in the kingdom of their Father. Whoever has ears, let them hear."
MATTHEW 13:43 NIV

I get it, Lord. You want me to keep my ears tuned in to Your still, small voice at all times—not just when I'm in need. Sure, You give me instructions for my own life, but You also long for me to reach out to others in tangible ways. So You give me gentle nudges. You whisper, *"That one needs your help."* You're the One who pointed me in the direction of the single mom. You're the One who reminded me to give online for that person with high medical bills. You're the One who encourages me daily to pray for that coworker who's going through a rough patch. I'm listening, Lord. With ears wide open, may I hear and obey. Amen.

BE THE CHANGE
Fill a freezer full of food for a family with a new baby.

Arise and Shine

"Arise, shine, for your light has come,
and the glory of the LORD rises upon you."
ISAIAH 60:1 NIV

It's hard to get moving when you've been still for so long. This I know from personal experience, Lord. I don't always want to leave the comfort of my sofa or my bed to help others, especially when I'm exhausted from daily living. I say things like, "Someone else will take care of it," or "This just isn't a good day for me." Then I'm reminded of the life of Your Son, how day after day He poured Himself out for those in need. I'm humbled by His willingness to keep going. May I learn from His example, Father. May I rouse myself from my slumber and hit the road running so I can impact this world for You. Amen.

BE THE CHANGE
Organize a clean-up party for a local park.

Courageous Faith

*Live wisely among those who are not believers,
and make the most of every opportunity.*
COLOSSIANS 4:5 NLT

Sometimes when I wonder how I can make a difference in the world, Lord, You remind me that standing up for what I believe is a key way to share the Gospel. I'm surrounded on every side by people—and circumstances—that contradict my faith. It's overwhelming at times because those who oppose me are so vocal, so loud. They shout their beliefs in my ears and insist on being heard. It's hard to take in. Sometimes I want to cower, to keep my mouth shut. But You're always opening doors for conversations, Lord, so I step right through them. With the courage of my convictions, help me to go on speaking truth in love, even when it's hard. Amen.

BE THE CHANGE
*Surprise your server with a large tip
the next time you go out to eat.*

A Mind Renewal

Do not be conformed to this world, but be transformed by the renewal of your mind, that by testing you may discern what is the will of God, what is good and acceptable and perfect.
ROMANS 12:2 ESV

I love the word *renewal*, Lord. It's fascinating to think that my mind can actually be made new. Sometimes I feel like I'm stuck in a rut. My mind seems to go along with whatever those around me are saying. But when I come to You—when I spend time in our secret places— You birth in me new ideas, new beliefs, new goals and dreams. You really do want to make all things new— even the things of my life, Father! That's why I'm tuning my ear in to You so that I can know Your will—not my neighbor's. I want to do the tasks You've set aside for me to do—not the things the world would have me accomplish. Thank You for renewing my heart and my mind, Lord. Amen.

BE THE CHANGE
Make a list of five times God changed your mind.

Rooted

And now, just as you accepted Christ Jesus as your Lord, you must continue to follow him. Let your roots grow down into him, and let your lives be built on him. Then your faith will grow strong in the truth you were taught, and you will overflow with thankfulness.
COLOSSIANS 2:6–7 NLT

I want to be rooted in You, Lord, so that I don't topple over when strong winds blow. I've noticed that my faith grows stronger during the hard seasons, and I know it's because I'm completely dependent on You, not on myself. This can only happen when my roots run deep—when I'm saturated with Your Word and life's situations are bathed in prayer. I'm also learning that people are watching my reactions to life's challenges. They want to know how a believer responds when the chips are down. When I'm rooted and grounded in You, I set a better example for others. So, today I choose to dig deep and to root myself in You. Amen.

BE THE CHANGE
Offer to drive a sick friend or neighbor to the doctor.

Firm but Loving

Be on your guard; stand firm in the faith;
be courageous; be strong. Do everything in love.
1 CORINTHIANS 16:13–14 NIV

I've got the firm thing down, Lord. I know how to rule
with an iron fist and have done so on many occasions
(sometimes hurting feelings in the process). But
tempering my firmness with love is a little harder. Your
Word instructs me to do everything in love. Everything, Lord? Even having tough conversations with
friends? Dealing with an unruly child? Talking to a bill
collector on the phone? Reacting to an erratic driver
on the road? Responding to a neighbor who doesn't
like my dog? This isn't an easy task, but I'll give it my
best shot because I know that others are watching.
They see when I knee-jerk. Help me, Father. May I
always be a reflection of You. Amen.

BE THE CHANGE
Offer to go to the grocery store for
someone who isn't feeling well.

No Shame Here

I am not ashamed of the gospel, for it is the power
of God for salvation to everyone who believes,
to the Jew first and also to the Greek.
ROMANS 1:16 ESV

Lord, I always tell people that I'm not ashamed of my
faith, but I wonder if I'm being totally honest. There
are times when I feel uncomfortable talking to others
about my beliefs, particularly those who don't get it.
They can be so unreceptive at times. This is especially
true when my faith and politics intertwine. Things can
get tricky, so I often keep my mouth shut. I don't want
to stir the waters. Show me how to rise above those
feelings of nervousness, Lord, so that I'm freed up to
share the Gospel message. I want to make a difference
in this world, Father, even when speaking the truth is
hard. Amen.

BE THE CHANGE
Volunteer at (or donate baby items to)
a local pregnancy assistance center.

To the Whole Creation

*He said to them, "Go into all the world and
proclaim the gospel to the whole creation."*
MARK 16:15 ESV

Lord, I don't mind admitting that this verse is a little
intimidating. There have been times when I've had
trouble crossing the street to talk to my neighbor
about my faith let alone traveling across the globe. I
know that You can and will use me in any situation, so
today I ask You to do just that. No matter where I am—
at work, at play, at home, or on a trip to the other side
of the world—You can speak through me to others.
It can happen in such a natural way that I don't even
have to wonder or worry about what I'll say. You open
doors of conversation with ease, Lord, and bid me
to walk through them. May I never forget that every
human being I come in contact with is one You died
to offer salvation to. When I remember that, talking
about You is so much easier. Amen.

BE THE CHANGE
Host a blanket drive for the homeless.

An Authentic Reflection

Above all else, you must live in a way that brings honor to the good news about Christ. Then, whether I visit you or not, I will hear that all of you think alike. I will know that you are working together and that you are struggling side by side to get others to believe the good news.
PHILIPPIANS 1:27 CEV

Lord, I want to be authentic. When people spend time with me in private, I want them to see the same person they see in public. No phony business. No hypocrisy. I want to bring honor to Your Name, in good times and in bad, in public and in private. I never want my faith to be a turnoff to those who are watching. Instead, I want them to be drawn to the Christ they see in me. Help me to live in a way that glorifies You, Father. I want to be a true reflection of You, to draw others into the kingdom. Amen.

BE THE CHANGE
Instead of saying, "I'll be praying for you," when a friend is in need, stop and pray for that person— right when and where you learn about the problem.

Always Prepared

*In your hearts honor Christ the Lord as holy, always being
prepared to make a defense to anyone who asks you
for a reason for the hope that is in you; yet do
it with gentleness and respect.*
1 PETER 3:15 ESV

It happens every now and again, Lord, that in the middle of a conversation with someone, I mention my faith and receive an unkind kickback about Christianity—or about You. I'm always caught off guard, Father. I suppose I think everyone will agree with me. . .but of course they don't. You've given us free will, and many use it to stay as far away from Christianity as possible. They have preconceived ideas that seem immovable. Still, I won't give up. I want to be ready—as this verse says—always prepared to make a defense for the hope that is in me. My testimony is a powerful tool, and I'm so excited to share it. Thanks for the opportunities. Amen.

BE THE CHANGE
Write down your testimony and share it with your children.

Being Bold

*"You will receive power when the Holy Spirit comes on you;
and you will be my witnesses in Jerusalem, and in all
Judea and Samaria, and to the ends of the earth."*
ACTS 1:8 NIV

I feel like such a weakling at times, Lord—like I don't
have an ounce of power inside of me. Then, just about
the time I'm ready to pull the covers over my head,
You rush in like a mighty wind and energize me as only
You can. The power that comes from Your Holy Spirit
is unlike anything humankind could ever manufac-
ture. I won't find it in a dietary supplement, an energy
drink, or even through exercise. That heaven-sent
power produces miraculous things, for it gives me the
courage to share my testimony. It also opens doors
and presents awesome opportunities for me to impact
lives. Thanks for this extra burst of boldness, Lord!
Amen.

BE THE CHANGE
*Invite a friend to a Christian concert or event. Offer to
drive so you can chat together about it on the way home.*

His Name Exalted

You will say in that day: "Give thanks to the Lord,
call upon his name, make known his deeds among
the peoples, proclaim that his name is exalted."
Isaiah 12:4 esv

Father, I can remember a time when it was safe to
speak Your Name publicly. I could talk about Your Son
openly and not just at Christmastime. Now it seems
that the Name of Jesus is politically incorrect and that
I'm being offensive when I greet others during the
holidays. I have no idea when this started, but it wears
me out! Why have people pushed You away, Lord? Your
Word is clear—Your Name is to be exalted. So I won't
back down. I'll keep proclaiming the precious saving
grace of Your Gospel message to all who will listen,
all year round. There's power in the Name of Jesus,
after all. Why would I ever cease to speak His Name?
I praise You, Lord. Amen.

Be the Change
Place a Jesus is the Reason for the Season!
sign in your yard during the holidays.

Unconditional Love

God shows his great love for us in this way:
Christ died for us while we were still sinners.
ROMANS 5:8 NCV

Lord, I've often pondered Your ability to love uncon-
ditionally. This "no matter what" approach to love
amazes me. How gracious You are to love even those
who don't love You, to serve those who don't show
appreciation, and to die on the cross for sinners like
me. All of this out of love. If I stumbled and fell, You
would cross many miles to reach me, Lord. But I'm not
alone. You have this same selfless love for people all
over the globe. You don't judge by skin color, by age,
or by personality type. You're truly a "One Love fits
all" Father. How grateful I am, Lord, for the unmerited
favor You've bestowed on me and the unconditional
love You've poured out. Amen.

BE THE CHANGE
Befriend someone who is your polar opposite.

Love Gives

"God so loved the world, that he gave his only Son, that whoever believes in him should not perish but have eternal life."
JOHN 3:16 ESV

I'll never understand how You did it, Father—how You sent Your only Son to the earth to die for mankind. What an amazing, selfless sacrifice He made, offering His life in exchange for sinners across the globe. I've learned so much from Your example. More than anything, I've discovered that love gives and gives and then gives some more. This sacrificial approach to life flies in the face of how most twenty-first-century people live. So many of us are in receiving mode, wanting our needs and wishes met (usually right away, thanks very much). But You've shown me that in order to bring about change in the world, I need to be a giver. Search my heart, Lord. Make me more like You. Amen.

BE THE CHANGE
Prepare a meal for a person in need or deliver Meals on Wheels to the elderly.

Giving Up Your Own Way

Then [Jesus] said to the crowd, "If any of you wants to be my follower, you must give up your own way, take up your cross daily, and follow me. If you try to hang on to your life, you will lose it. But if you give up your life for my sake, you will save it."
LUKE 9:23–24 NLT

I'll be honest, Lord—I haven't always been a fan of the words "give up your own way." I'm more accustomed to insisting on my own way than giving it up. But You're reversing my way of thinking. It's not "my way or the highway." It's Your way, Father, so that all might come to know You because (in part) of my selfless example of what it means to be a believer. This may take some work on my part. It won't come naturally. But I'm in this for the long haul, Lord. Keep transforming my heart and my thoughts, I pray, that I may come to see people through Your eyes. Amen.

BE THE CHANGE
Bake and deliver sweet treats to your local police officers or firefighters.

Wishing Others Well

*Wish good for those who harm you; wish them well
and do not curse them. Be happy with those who
are happy, and be sad with those who are sad.*
ROMANS 12:14–15 NCV

Lord, if I want to bring about change in this world, I
need to adjust my thinking. Instead of getting angry
or bitter when people hurt me, I need to follow the
advice in this scripture. It's not easy to wish them
well, especially in the heat of the battle, but I want my
heart to beat in sync with Yours, and You're a lover not
a hater. So change my stinking thinking, Father. Shift
my desired response to blessing not cursing. Make
me a giver not a taker. I want to be known as one who
truly cares about others, even those who've done me
wrong. Help me, I pray. Amen.

BE THE CHANGE
*Send a card or letter of encouragement
to someone who has wounded you.*

Joined Together

I beg you, brothers and sisters, by the name of our Lord Jesus Christ that all of you agree with each other and not be split into groups. I beg that you be completely joined together by having the same kind of thinking and the same purpose.
1 CORINTHIANS 1:10 NCV

This is a hard one, Lord. I'm so accustomed to hanging out with those who agree with me. We usually just avoid the ones who disagree. Life is easier this way. But You didn't call me to an easy life, did You? After all, it's hard to be unified with people I'm not even attempting to get along with. Soften my heart toward those who have a different mind-set. Help me to love them in spite of our differences. And while You're at it, please soften their hearts too. I long to live at peace with all of my brothers and sisters, bringing joy to Your heart as we walk in unity. Thanks in advance for the work You're going to do, Lord. Amen.

BE THE CHANGE
Offer to help clean up after an event.

Led by Love

*Let love be your guide. Christ loved us and offered
his life for us as a sacrifice that pleases God.*
EPHESIANS 5:2 CEV

I want love to be my guide, Lord. I don't want to chase
after anything else. I wouldn't go trekking off into
the wilderness without a compass; neither would I
try to navigate this life without love. It leads the way
as nothing else can. Love clears a path better than
any weed trimmer. It barrels through brush, protects
from injury, and shines a light on the path so that I
know which way to go. This is especially helpful when
darkness seems to be invading the earth. More than
anything, love unifies. It binds me to others around
me—those I'm like and those who are vastly different.
Show me how to love as You love, Lord. Amen.

BE THE CHANGE

*Offer a one-day car-care clinic for single moms
or elderly citizens in your community.*

While We Were Yet Sinners

But you, O Lord, are a God merciful and gracious, slow to anger and abounding in steadfast love and faithfulness.
PSALM 86:15 ESV

You didn't wait until I had my act together to whisper, *"I love you"* in my ear, did You, Lord? No, You made Your feelings known while I was still a mess, before I ever attempted to clean myself up. Some of my friends and family members are a mess, Lord. They're not interested in hearing about You. Many seem content in their bondage. I haven't quite figured out how to reach out to them. I don't want to put a stamp of approval on their lifestyles, but neither do I want to push them away. Show me how to follow Your example, Lord—how to show the kind of love that leads to repentance. I need Your help with this one, Father. Amen.

BE THE CHANGE
Cover someone's library fines.

Paid in Full

*Let no debt remain outstanding, except
the continuing debt to love one another,
for whoever loves others has fulfilled the law.*
ROMANS 13:8 NIV

Father, I don't want to leave this life with any outstanding debts. I don't want to owe time, talents, or treasures to You or anyone else I care about. Most of all, I don't want to leave without letting people know how much I love them. I don't always show it to those outside my family, and, I'll confess, I don't always show it to those *inside* my family either. But I don't want to leave any room for doubt in people's minds, so show me how to share love in a way that makes each individual feel wanted and appreciated. I want to pay this love debt in full, Father. Amen.

BE THE CHANGE
Send a card to a loved one (of your choice) today.

A Blanket of Love

Above all, keep loving one another earnestly,
since love covers a multitude of sins.
1 PETER 4:8 ESV

There have been so many times in my life when I've
messed up, Lord. I've said the wrong thing, done the
wrong thing, or made the wrong decision. But in every
case You've covered my transgressions/errors with
Your great blanket of love. It truly does cover a multitude of sins (and insults and bitterness and pain). Show
me how to use this blanket to mend broken relationships, I pray. I long for healing—between friends, family
members, and coworkers. Your Word says love is the
greatest gift of all, so today, with Your help, I offer it
to those I've hurt, so that I might find myself walking
in relationship with them once again. Amen.

BE THE CHANGE
Show Christ's love to someone who has
treated you in an unloving way.

The Peace of Christ

Let the peace of Christ rule in your hearts, to which indeed you were called in one body; and be thankful.
COLOSSIANS 3:15 NASB

Oh how I love this verse, Lord! It's Your peace I want—not the so-called peace the world offers. When I allow Your peace to rule my heart, I'm completely content. I don't question every little thing. I'm not uneasy all the time or wondering if I made the right decisions. I'm truly resting in You because I know You have my best interests at heart. This same peace helps me to live in community with others and avoid quarreling when we don't share the same opinions or deeply held beliefs. Somehow, You cover it all. What a great peacemaker You are, Lord! Amen.

BE THE CHANGE
Offer to drive an elderly friend or neighbor to the grocery store.

Random Acts of Kindness

*But the fruit of the Spirit is love, joy, peace,
patience, kindness, goodness, faithfulness.*
GALATIANS 5:22 ESV

Random acts of kindness. They're so fun, Lord! I love
dreaming up all sorts of ideas—things I can do to
bless kids, grown-ups, elderly people, friends, family
members, coaches, teachers, the clerk at the super-
market, or even strangers. I want to bless them all
with unexpected encouragement and surprises. They
all need Your touch and a reminder that they are not
alone. I need Your help to come up with creative ideas.
What a great time we're going to have—You and me—
dreaming up cool things to let these amazing people
know You haven't forgotten them. Let's get started,
Lord! Amen.

BE THE CHANGE
Surprise a stranger by paying for a tank of gas.

A Hope and a Blessing

*Do not let kindness and truth leave you; bind them
around your neck, write them on the tablet of your heart.*
PROVERBS 3:3 NASB

God, I get it now! The very best way to bless others
is to make kindness and truth an everyday part of my
life. When my heart is softened toward others, when I
genuinely care about their needs, I'll bring hope to the
hopeless, love to those feeling unloved. My greatest
desire will be to bless them. I'm filled with so many
ideas, dreaming up so many different ways I can bring
hope. When others see me, I want them to say, "Wow!
That one's really got a heart for others!" With Your
help, I will be that sort of person, Lord. Amen.

BE THE CHANGE
Collect blankets for a women's shelter.

Serving One Another

As each has received a gift, use it to serve one
another, as good stewards of God's varied grace.
1 PETER 4:10 ESV

I like to be the boss, Lord. Just put me in charge and
I'll do my best work, especially if others are watching.
No one will question the decision to place me in lead-
ership. But You're teaching me that it's best to humble
myself and take on the role of servant at times, to
care about the desires of others, and to make sure
their needs are met. Today I choose to change my
world by tuning in, by paying attention to what's going
on in the lives of those around me. When I'm in touch
with their needs, I know how to pray. And maybe, just
maybe, You'll show me how to meet some of those
needs in tangible ways without being the top guy on
the totem pole. Amen.

BE THE CHANGE
Send cards to soldiers serving overseas.

Overflowing with Hope

*May the God of hope fill you with all joy and
peace as you trust in him, so that you may
overflow with hope by the power of the Holy Spirit.*
ROMANS 15:13 NIV

I know what the word *overflowing* looks like, Lord.
I've seen it a few times: when taking a bath, washing
dishes, and running the dishwasher. I even saw hints
of it during a recent rainstorm! To some, *overflow*
means "too much." But when it comes to extending
love and hope to others, Father, it's impossible to go
overboard. You want me to overflow with hope in
every situation, to completely trust in You even when
things seem impossible. When I live a lifestyle of hope,
others will see it and want to put their hope in You too,
Lord. So fill me to the tip-top, and then let my hope
overflow! Amen.

BE THE CHANGE
Give a gift card to someone you care about.

Hope Brings Peace

*Jesus said to them again, "Peace be with you.
As the Father has sent me, even so I am sending you."*
JOHN 20:21 ESV

It makes sense, Lord. When my hope is high, my peace rises too. I'm not fretting and worrying about what tomorrow might bring, so I'm calm, cool, and collected. That's the benefit of trusting in You. I want to share that hope so others can be peaceful too. Many of the people I know—friends, loved ones, family members—seem hopeless. You sent Your Son to bring hope to the world, and now You're sending me to do the same. What an awesome task, and how honored I am to be chosen by You, Lord. May all come to fully know the hope and peace that only You can bring. Amen.

BE THE CHANGE

*Adopt a grandparent you can treat as your own—
with all of the affection a grandparent deserves!*

Welcome to the Neighborhood!

Lord, where do I put my hope?
My only hope is in you.
PSALM 39:7 NLT

Here's a fun idea, Lord: I could be a welcome committee to new people moving into my neighborhood. Give me creative ideas so that I can make my new neighbors feel right at home, as soon as they move in. I know what it feels like to be the new kid in town. It's awkward, at best. But open arms and a few welcoming words should do the trick. I can learn from You, Lord. You welcomed me into Your neighborhood with open arms, after all. You swept me into the fold and made me part of the family, brushing away all feelings of awkwardness. May I learn from Your example, I pray. Amen.

BE THE CHANGE
Head up the welcome committee in your neighborhood.

Tree of Life

Hope deferred makes the heart sick,
but a dream fulfilled is a tree of life.
PROVERBS 13:12 NLT

I love the image of a "tree of life," Lord. That's what I want to be to all those I come in contact with. I want to spread my branches wide—to offer hope to my neighbors who are hurting, loved ones going through tough stuff, and friends in need. Show me how to deepen my roots in You, Father, that I might stand strong during difficult seasons, even in my own life, and see them through to dream fulfillment. I want to make a difference in this world by being sturdy, healthy, and dependable. I praise You for growing me into one who is usable in the kingdom, Lord. Amen.

BE THE CHANGE

Plan a neighborhood cookout. Invite everyone on
your block for an afternoon of fun and friendship.

His Name Brings Hope

"His name will be the hope of all the world."
MATTHEW 12:21 NLT

Lord, there's so much power in Your Name! When I speak the Name of Jesus, demons have to flee. Mountains move. Prayers are answered. Lives are transformed for all eternity. Your Name brings hope—not just to my circumstances, not just to those I love, but to people around the world. That's why the enemy is trying so hard to squelch the Name of Jesus, because he knows there's power in that Name. But I'll go on shouting, "Praise You, Jesus!" at the top of my lungs and watch as miracles take place. What an awesome, holy Name that I'm proud to share with the world. Amen.

BE THE CHANGE
Make and send care packages to men and women in the military. For that added sense of community, put them together with your neighbors or people you're trying to get to know.

The Source of Hope

*I pray that God, the source of hope, will fill you completely with
joy and peace because you trust in him. Then you will overflow
with confident hope through the power of the Holy Spirit.*
ROMANS 15:13 NLT

Many times in my life, I've tried to tap into people or
things to bring hope. Friends. Family members. Jobs.
Activities. Hobbies. But You've been teaching me an
important lesson, Lord: I'll always come up empty un-
less I tap into You, the True Source of hope. Oh, those
other things will lift my spirits for a short season, but if
I want long-term hope, I need to stay plugged in to the
Author of hope. You completely fill me, top to bottom,
with a hope that doesn't fade after a few hours or
days. Today, Father, I place my trust in You once again.
I praise You for the hope You bring. Amen.

BE THE CHANGE

*Bring hope to a teacher at a local school
by offering to help set up the classroom
before the start of a new school year.*

The Inner Sanctuary

This hope is a strong and trustworthy anchor for our souls.
It leads us through the curtain into God's inner sanctuary.
HEBREWS 6:19 NLT

I want to go deep with You, Lord. No surface relationships here! I'm so grateful You've invited me to the inner sanctuary, the Holy of Holies, a place where I can truly commune with You. There, in that holy place, I find the true anchor for my soul. I don't have to rely on my own strength when I'm with You. You extend Your arms and say, *"Rest awhile in me."* When I take the time to do that, miraculous things happen. My hope is restored. I'm energized inside out. I'm refreshed, renewed, and ready to impact the world once again. Oh how I love Your presence, Father. Where else can I find such joy, peace, and life? Amen.

BE THE CHANGE
Be authentic in your relationships. Spend
quality time with a friend or loved one today.

The Golden Rule

"Do to others as you would have them do to you."
LUKE 6:31 NIV

I must confess, Lord, sometimes I want to say, "Do to others," and leave off the "as you would have them do to you" part. I can get more interested in personal justice than personal sacrifice. But You are making me see things from Your perspective, and that means I have to care as much about others as I do about myself if I want to change this world. So, Father, I'll treat others according to the Golden Rule—as I would want to be treated myself. If I truly live that way, people will be drawn to me and, as a result, drawn to You. It's a win-win situation when I follow Your lead. Thank You, Lord. Amen.

BE THE CHANGE
Offer to help a friend with a garage sale.

Others Before Self

Make me completely happy! Live in harmony by showing love for each other. Be united in what you think, as if you were only one person.
PHILIPPIANS 2:2 CEV

Putting others before myself flies in the face of how I normally live, Lord. I want what I want when I want it. If I'm hungry I eat. If I'm cold I grab a coat or blanket. If I'm uncomfortable I do whatever I can to rectify the situation, because comfort is my best friend. If my shoes are pinching my toes, I simply buy a new pair. Problem solved! I see that You're shifting my gaze to others a lot these days though. That homeless man who's shivering in the cold? I can give him a blanket. That woman in the shelter who's hungry? I can help feed her. That child without shoes? I can purchase a pair. There are so many things I can do to put others ahead of myself. Give me creative ideas, I pray. Amen.

BE THE CHANGE
Donate blood.

Loving One Another

Beloved, if God so loved us,
we also ought to love one another.
1 JOHN 4:11 ESV

This is such a simple command: love one another.
And I do my best, Lord (though some people are
tougher to love than others). I want a change of perspective so that I can see people the way You do.
I know that Your supernatural love extends to all,
even the most heinous. The man behind bars for that
horrible crime? You died for him. That woman who
abuses her child? You still love her in spite of her
actions. That white-collar boss who defrauded his own
workers? You adore him. I'll never fully understand it,
but I want to try. Show me how to love others "in spite
of." Then give me ideas for how to show that love—
whether to inmates in prison or simply people who are
different than me. I'm excited to learn, Lord. Amen.

BE THE CHANGE
Volunteer at a homeless shelter.

The Significance of Others

Do nothing from selfish ambition or conceit, but in humility count others more significant than yourselves.
PHILIPPIANS 2:3 ESV

I've been thinking about the word *significant*, Lord. I don't mind admitting that I want to feel that way—like I have value, like I matter. It has occurred to me that I'm not alone. Everyone longs to feel this way, and I can aid in their quest. That woman who has been battered by her husband and made to feel like she's not worthy of love? I can love her. That man who lost job after job and wonders if he'll ever be able to provide for his family? I can pray for him and provide Christmas gifts for his kids. That child who feels he'll never amount to anything? I can tutor him. You're giving me all sorts of ideas for how I can make others feel significant. When I'm focused on "them," "me" isn't at the front of my mind. It's a lovely way to live, Lord. Amen.

BE THE CHANGE
Become an ambassador for a missionary whose great work you want to tell others about.

When We Pause to Look

"A Samaritan, as he traveled, came where the man was;
and when he saw him, he took pity on him."
LUKE 10:33 NIV

I love this tale of the Good Samaritan, Lord. My
favorite part of the story? He stopped to examine
the situation, to give it a closer look. Others marched
right by and even crossed the street. They didn't care
to see, because seeing would require action on their
part. But this guy made a conscious decision to look
closer. He paused and took inventory. How many
times have I rushed by someone in need, shifting my
gaze to the other side of the road? More times than I
can count. But no more. I want to be known as a giver,
Lord, someone who pays attention. So, redirect my
thoughts. Open my eyes wider than ever to see those
in need around me. Give me Your vision, I pray. Amen.

BE THE CHANGE
Create goody bags for the homeless
and keep them in your car.

It Matters to God

*The LORD tests the righteous, but his soul hates
the wicked and the one who loves violence.*
PSALM 11:5 ESV

How I treat others matters to You, Lord. I know You
care about how I respond to loved ones, coworkers,
friends, and so on, but You're also watching how I
treat the seemingly invisible in my society—the single
moms, the elderly, the outcasts, the ones with chronic
illnesses. You care deeply about them all. You're
waiting to see me play a role in caring for those less
fortunate—whether I'll step up and be Your hands and
feet in my community. Today I recommit myself to this
task. May I be known as one who genuinely cares and
works hard to make a difference. Amen.

BE THE CHANGE
Read to residents at a nursing home or rehab hospital.

The "All of You" Group

Finally, all of you, be like-minded, be sympathetic,
love one another, be compassionate and humble.
1 PETER 3:8 NIV

All of you. Wow. I get it, Lord. There was a time when I thought only a handful of people were called by You to care for the needy, the down-and-out. Missionaries, evangelists, pastors—these were the ones I held responsible for tending to the homeless, the indigent, the ill. But You've convinced me, Father! I'm part of the "all of you" group, and it's my job to make a difference in the lives of people in need. Show me how to link arms with local and foreign ministries so that I can be effective. Use me in ways You've never used me before. I give myself to Your service, Father. Amen.

BE THE CHANGE

Offer to help a local or foreign missions organization. Perhaps you can send out a newsletter, raise funds, or host a drive.

Competitive Strides

Love one another with brotherly affection.
Outdo one another in showing honor.
ROMANS 12:10 ESV

This is a fun concept, Lord! You want us to outdo one another—not with our talents or treasures but in showing honor to each other. We're accustomed to being in competition mode, but our motives are usually self-focused. It'll be fun to try this new approach. Opening doors for people. Offering an empathetic smile or helping hand to a young mom with a rowdy toddler. Helping an elderly person manage a walker. Bringing a meal to a family when one member is in the hospital. There are so many little ways I can show love and honor to someone every day. My imagination is in overdrive just thinking about it. I can't wait to get started. Continue to give me ideas, I pray. Amen.

BE THE CHANGE
Take a meal to a single mom.

Purified by You

*Having purified your souls by your obedience
to the truth for a sincere brotherly love,
love one another earnestly from a pure heart.*
1 PETER 1:22 ESV

I know what it means to be purified, Lord. I've heard
how gold is purified in fire. (I love this imagery!) It's
not always easy to go through the purification process,
especially as it pertains to my relationships, but I'll give
it my best shot. I know that I'll only impact the lives of
others if they actually want to be around me, so I sub-
mit myself to this process so that I may learn to be a
true and lasting friend. Show me how to earnestly love
others, no matter who they are or what they've done.
Purify my heart, I pray. May all of the dross fall off, and
let only what's holy remain. Amen.

BE THE CHANGE
Host a food drive for the needy.

Each Part Working Properly

From whom the whole body, joined and held together
by every joint with which it is equipped, when each
part is working properly, makes the body grow
so that it builds itself up in love.
EPHESIANS 4:16 ESV

Lord, there have been times when I've been in a group setting and things didn't go well. Too many personalities at play caused friction and bad feelings. These situations are uncomfortable. Still, I know You long for us to live at peace with others. So today I choose to pray for those in my group instead of complaining about them. I pray for peace, of course, but I also pray that each individual would be fully devoted to You and to each other. When every part is working properly, we will make a strong team, ready to take on the world. Bring healing to every part, I pray. Amen.

BE THE CHANGE

Be willing to be a part of the group not the leader.

Peer Pressure

*Don't take part in doing those worthless things that are
done in the dark. Instead, show how wrong they are. It is
disgusting even to talk about what is done in the dark.*
EPHESIANS 5:11–12 CEV

I've given in to it, Lord. Peer pressure. It's such a
subtle, manipulative thing. One minute I'm convinced
no one can talk me into doing something I know is
wrong; the next I'm all in, doing what my peers are
doing. This is especially true when it comes to gossiping about others or cutting mutual friends down when
their backs are turned. I don't mean to do it. Somehow, I get sucked in. I'm always so ashamed afterward.
I vow to do better next time. This time I really mean
it. I need Your help, Lord. Whenever my friends start
up with the usual gossip, give me the courage to back
away. Amen.

BE THE CHANGE
Send a card to someone who's hurting.

No Bullying!

Whoever walks with the wise becomes wise,
but the companion of fools will suffer harm.
PROVERBS 13:20 ESV

Bullies drive me crazy, Lord! It doesn't matter if they're kids on the playground picking on my child or if they're adults in the workplace vying to take down a fellow employee. You know what it feels like to be abused and rejected, Lord. Your Son went through every emotion when He came to the earth to die for mankind. He somehow managed to love the bullies, even when they hung Him on a cross. I'll never know how He was able to look down and say, "Father, forgive them, for they know not what they do" (Luke 23:34 ESV), but I want to learn from His example. Help me to put a stop to bullying by vowing not to participate. And help me to protect those who are most vulnerable to bullying. I want to make a difference, Lord. Amen.

BE THE CHANGE
Include those who are rarely included.

Prejudice

*Do not conform to the pattern of this world,
but be transformed by the renewing of your mind.
Then you will be able to test and approve what
God's will is—his good, pleasing and perfect will.*
ROMANS 12:2 NIV

Some people look different, Lord. They don't fit in.
They speak a different language or dress a different
way. Their skin color is different. They're from a
different culture, one I'm not familiar with. Many are
struggling to find their way, and those in my inner
circle haven't done much to help. Today, please
show me how I can combat prejudice not just in my
neighborhood, my church, or my town but in general.
When You look at us, You don't see people divided by
languages and cultures; You see one big happy family.
And it is Your will that we see this too. Show me how
I can play a role in making people feel like they fit in,
I pray. Amen.

BE THE CHANGE
*Offer to change someone's porch
light or smoke detector batteries.*

The Real Deal

If anyone says, "I love God," and hates his brother,
he is a liar; for he who does not love his brother whom
he has seen cannot love God whom he has not seen.
1 John 4:20 ESV

I have to confess, I'm not always who I pretend to be,
Lord. Sometimes I'm sweet to people to their faces
but snarl when they look away. I tolerate. I put up with.
But I don't really love. I fake it because I want to look
godly when others are watching. But when I turn the
other way, the real me comes out. Oops. You don't
like this kind of hypocrisy. I know that, Lord. So please
help me. I want to be the same person when I turn
away from a conversation as I was when chatting face-
to-face. I'll be a "real deal" friend. You take this kind of
love very seriously, I know, so help me, I pray. Amen.

Be the Change
Send an encouraging message to someone
who's been feeling on the fringes.

No Cause to Stumble

*Let's stop condemning each other. Decide instead
to live in such a way that you will not cause
another believer to stumble and fall.*
ROMANS 14:13 NLT

This is a tough one, Lord! Sometimes I can be pretty
critical. I see the flaws in others and feel the need to
point them out. My words bring discouragement to
others at times, sometimes to folks who are trying
really hard to do the right thing. I'm sorry I get like
this, Father. I don't want to be the sort of person who
causes others to stumble. I long to be an encourager,
not a discourager. When I get to heaven, I don't want
to see a long line of people who struggled on my
account. Instead, I want to see a chain of people who
were impacted in a positive way by my kindness and
generosity. Help me with this, I pray. Amen.

BE THE CHANGE
Offer to help change someone's tire.

God Pleaser

Am I now seeking the approval of man, or of God?
Or am I trying to please man? If I were still trying
to please man, I would not be a servant of Christ.
GALATIANS 1:10 ESV

I want to please You, Lord, but I confess there are times I'm more interested in pleasing the people around me. I say yes to things I should say no to because I want people to like me. I try extra hard to fit in because acceptance feels good. I bend over backward and get in over my head with projects because I want to seen as a worker bee—someone others can depend on. This isn't always Your will, Father. Sometimes You want me to back away, to say no, to spend more time in Your presence. If I've drifted into any co-dependent relationships, Lord, please show me how to undo the damage I've done. From now on, I will seek to please You not the people around me. Amen.

BE THE CHANGE
Do a good deed in secret.

Resisting Temptation

My son, if sinful men entice you,
do not give in to them.
PROVERBS 1:10 NIV

Temptation is hard, Lord! There have been times I've felt like I was hanging on by my fingertips—unwilling to give in. Then other times I've released my hold on my faith and tumbled headfirst into sin. I don't want to be one who gives in easily. I want to go down kicking and screaming when temptation comes my way. Guard me from relationships that pull me away from You. I want to impact my world, and that means I will sometimes end up hanging out with people who don't know You yet; but I don't ever want to compromise my faith or give up on what I know to be true. Guard my heart and my spirit, I pray. Amen.

BE THE CHANGE
Offer to pray for someone who is hurting.

Not a Fool

Don't fool yourselves.
Bad friends will destroy you.
1 CORINTHIANS 15:33 CEV

I've had the privilege of sharing Your Gospel message with others, Lord. I love to tell people young and old what a difference You've made in my life. How wonderful when they respond by putting their trust in You! It's an amazing feeling to know that someone has entered Your family as a result of my witness, my testimony. May I continue to influence others in a positive way instead falling into the old trap of being influenced by the sinful lifestyle of others. I don't want to go backward—ever. I pray for only forward movement from this point on. I've come too far to slip into old patterns. And I want to bring as many to heaven with me as I can. Thanks for helping me, Lord. Amen.

BE THE CHANGE
Host an after-school program
at a local elementary school.

Held

*"Do not fear, for I am with you; do not be dismayed,
for I am your God. I will strengthen you and help you;
I will uphold you with my righteous right hand."*
ISAIAH 41:10 NIV

There are times when I feel Your presence so keenly,
Lord. This is especially true during hard seasons. If Your
hand didn't hold me up, I would surely hit the ground.
Defeat would set in. How precious to realize You love
me enough to hold me, no matter what I'm going
through. You're working out an amazing testimony in
my life. Others will be encouraged when they hear
what You have done. I know You're doing the same
thing in their lives too. We would surely give up if not
for Your intervention, Father. What a good and loving
Father You are! Amen.

BE THE CHANGE

*Share your testimony on social media. Let the
world know what God has done in Your life.*

The Whole World

"What will it profit a man if he gains the whole world and forfeits his soul? Or what shall a man give in return for his soul?"
MATTHEW 16:26 ESV

Sometimes I feel like that little girl in the movie *Willy Wonka & the Chocolate Factory*, Lord. I find myself saying, "I want it, and I want it *now!*" Then I'm reminded that getting what I wish for isn't always for the best. What good would it do me to receive all that I ever longed for, only to lose my soul? Life isn't about stuff. It's about loving You and being loved in return. It's about losing my life so that I can find it in You. It's about sharing the joy of my journey with You. May I never exchange any of that for the temporary pleasures life can bring, Lord. It's not worth it, and I'm glad I've figured that out. Amen.

BE THE CHANGE
That very thing you've been wishing and longing for? Buy it and give it to a friend.

Perfect Harmony

*Above all, clothe yourselves with love,
which binds us all together in perfect harmony.*
COLOSSIANS 3:14 NLT

Lord, this is a big, wide world filled with people of
every race and creed. When I think about all of us
living together in harmony, it feels impossible. There
are those, after all, who oppose all that I believe in and
stand for. We're polar opposites. As much as I'm able
though, I want to live at peace with others. This will
only happen if I approach people with love. Perhaps, if
I love my way through, I'll impact lives with the Gospel
message. And when it comes to my fellow believers,
Lord, may I always seek to live in harmony. We're
brothers and sisters, after all! Amen.

BE THE CHANGE
Take a new friend to lunch or dinner.

Good Measure

"Give, and it will be given to you. Good measure, pressed down,
shaken together, running over, will be put into your lap. For
with the measure you use it will be measured back to you."
LUKE 6:38 ESV

I remember once at a butcher shop, Lord, watching as
the butcher put a bit more meat on the scale than I'd
asked for. He wrapped it up anyway and didn't charge
me for the excess. That's how it is when I serve You.
You're always giving me more than I expect. You're
a generous God! And I see now that You want me
to have that same generous spirit. When I give, you
give back—good measure (like the butcher!). Pressed
down, shaken together, running over—that's how You
weigh things, Father. Have I mentioned how grateful I
am for Your generosity? I praise You, Lord. Amen.

BE THE CHANGE
Pay for someone's medication.

Caring for the Disabled

*If anyone is poor among your fellow Israelites in any of
the towns of the land the L*ORD *your God is giving you,
do not be hardhearted or tightfisted toward them. Rather,
be openhanded and freely lend them whatever they need.*
DEUTERONOMY 15:7–8 NIV

Lord, I want to do a better job of reaching out to the
disabled in my community. There are times when
I'm at a complete loss about how I can help. So, I do
nothing. I stick to the fringes and let other people
take over. But You're giving me creative ideas! I can
volunteer in a special needs classroom. I can take care
of a friend's disabled child for a few hours. I can take a
meal to a caregiver so there's one less thing to worry
about. I can offer to clean the home of a person who's
hospitalized so it's ready to return to. I want to be
openhanded toward people, Lord—not just those who
are easy to minister to but everyone. Please give me
Your heart and Your attitude toward those who are
disabled. Amen.

BE THE CHANGE
Help a caregiver with a special meal or dessert.

Caring More and More

*This is my prayer for you: that your love
will grow more and more; that you will have
knowledge and understanding with your love.*
PHILIPPIANS 1:9 NCV

I don't always jump up and down when needs are
presented, Lord. Sometimes my "want to" is missing.
But You tug at my heartstrings, and I begin to care.
That's the thing about You that amazes me most, Lord:
You can take my hard heart and soften it. Before long,
I become passionate on behalf of people in need. I become a spokesperson for the disabled or an advocate
for children with autism. I become passionate about
caregivers who tend to those with Alzheimer's disease
or feel eager to get the word out about neuromus-
cular diseases. In other words, in Your pliable hands,
I care more and more with each passing day. Only
You could accomplish that in my heart, Lord. I'm so
grateful. Amen.

BE THE CHANGE
Provide toiletries for a local shelter.

Caring for Shut-Ins

Bear one another's burdens,
and so fulfill the law of Christ.
GALATIANS 6:2 ESV

Some folks aren't able to tend to their own needs,
Lord. They're completely dependent on others. I
can't imagine what that must feel like, though I try.
These poor souls may be confined to their homes
most of the time. Homebound. Show me how I can
reach out to someone in such a situation. Should I
visit? Offer to tidy up or cook meals? Perhaps I
should offer to run errands, sort through medications,
or provide transport to medical appointments?
There's got to be something I can do to help make
the days more agreeable. Show me, I pray. Amen.

BE THE CHANGE

Go grocery shopping with or
for a disabled neighbor or friend.

Caring for the Grieving

*"He will wipe away every tear from their eyes,
and there will be no more death, sadness, crying,
or pain, because all the old ways are gone."*
REVELATION 21:4 NCV

I don't know how to help loved ones through pain,
Lord, through suffering. Grief can be intense. I stand
next to precious friends or loved ones, wishing I
knew how to take the pain away. I try to speak words
of consolation, but they fall short. Show me how to
be a comfort, Lord. May the peace of Your Son ring
through my words. May those who are grieving feel
Your presence in my hugs. May they come to know the
depth of my caring as I bring meals or whisper prayers.
More than anything, I want these precious friends to
know they are not alone, not forgotten. Help me, I
pray. Amen.

BE THE CHANGE

*If your friend or loved one is hosting family members who
are in town for a funeral, be present. Bring paper products.
Set up a meal train. Help with dishes and house cleaning.*

Caring for the Sick

Is anyone among you suffering? Let him pray. Is anyone cheerful? Let him sing praise. Is anyone among you sick? Let him call for the elders of the church, and let them pray over him, anointing him with oil in the name of the Lord. And the prayer of faith will save the one who is sick, and the Lord will raise him up. And if he has committed sins, he will be forgiven.
JAMES 5:13–15 ESV

I'm heartbroken for those who suffer with illnesses, Lord. Whether they have chronic conditions or find themselves in dire straits in the hospital with unexpected infections or cancer, my heart prickles. I want to help. My prayers are steadfast, and I visit as often as I can, but show me what else I can do to ease the suffering. Can I tend to children? Bring communion to the hospital? Relieve weary caregivers for a night? I want to be of service, but I don't want to get in the way. Show me how I can make others' seasons of suffering better for them, I pray. Amen.

BE THE CHANGE
*Offer to take an elderly friend
to a doctor's appointment.*

As You Care for Yourself

*Jesus replied: "'Love the Lord your God with all
your heart and with all your soul and with all your
mind.' This is the first and greatest commandment.
And the second is like it: 'Love your neighbor as yourself.'"*
MATTHEW 22:37–39 NIV

I wonder how things would be, Lord, if I were the one
in great need. Would friends and loved ones rush to
my aid? Would provision be made for every detail,
even the smallest one? I want to tend to those who
are struggling in the same way I hope and pray they
would care for my needs. I want to be there so they
never forget that someone cares. Show me how to
be the best possible friend to people in dire circumstances, Father. I want to love others through their
deepest valleys. Please help me as I try. Amen.

BE THE CHANGE
*Raise funds for a hurting family's
mortgage payment or utility bills.*

The Household of Faith

*As we have opportunity, let us do good to everyone,
and especially to those who are of the household of faith.*
GALATIANS 6:10 ESV

The body of Christ is my family, Lord. I've got brothers
and sisters by the hundreds. I'm particularly thrilled
to be part of a Christian community near where I live.
My church, my Christian friends—they mean the world
to me. I want to keep my ear attuned to the needs of
those in my circle. I don't want to find out after-the-
fact that a family was in need and no one swept in to
help. May I be the one to sweep in. So open my ears,
Lord. Help me to hear. Open my eyes. Help me to see.
May I never overlook a fellow believer who's going
through a rough season. May I always be the kind of
friend to offer a shoulder and a hand. Amen.

BE THE CHANGE
Donate to your church's food pantry.

Caring for Orphans and Widows

*Religion that is pure and undefiled before God
the Father is this: to visit orphans and widows in their
affliction, and to keep oneself unstained from the world.*
JAMES 1:27 ESV

This is the proof of my religion, Lord: taking care of orphans and widows. It's not a suggestion on Your part; it's a mandate—one that I don't always remember. I'm so grateful for the reminder through this verse that You care deeply about the defenseless. You're a defender of the weak, and You're making me want to be a defender too. May I stand up when others seek to bring harm. May I help where help is needed, feed where food is needed, and provide care where care is needed. In other words, I want to do the right thing so that these precious ones know they are never, ever alone. Amen.

BE THE CHANGE
*Host Thanksgiving dinner for
a widow or family in need.*

Caring for the Animal Kingdom

The righteous care for the needs of their animals,
but the kindest acts of the wicked are cruel.
PROVERBS 12:10 NIV

I'm a fan of animals, Lord. I love puppies, kittens, and many other species besides. They bring great joy to my heart. I know that many are mistreated or in less-than-stellar situations. Please give me creative ideas to help out at my local shelter. Should I donate food, funds, or other items? Offer to walk the dogs? Clean out kitties' cages? Bathe the pups? Or am I ready to adopt an elderly cat or a dog in need? I know that You care very deeply about animals. The story of Noah and the ark convinces me of that. So, help me to do my best to take care of the animal kingdom so that I might make Your heart happy. Amen.

BE THE CHANGE
Offer to babysit the pet(s) of a friend
or neighbor who is going out of town.

Prayer Moves Mountains

*"Watch and pray so that you will not fall into temptation.
The spirit is willing, but the flesh is weak."*
MATTHEW 26:41 NIV

Father, Your Word tells me that prayer can move
mountains. When I pray, my words have power. There
are many mountains in my life I'd love to see moved:
depression, financial woes, relationship issues, and
so on. So today I stare those obstacles down and say,
"Be gone, in Jesus' Name!" From now on, I'll pray in
faith. I won't get discouraged by how big my problem
is; instead, I'll tell my problem how big God is. When I
speak in faith, I will encourage both myself and those
around me. Situations can and will change with just
a few faith-filled words. How I praise You for that!
Amen.

BE THE CHANGE

*Offer to pray in faith with a friend
who's going through a rough season.*

Praying for the World

There is neither Jew nor Gentile, neither slave nor free, nor is there male and female, for you are all one in Christ Jesus.
GALATIANS 3:28 NIV

Father, this world is filled with billions of people, most of whom are nothing like me. Their homes are different, their foods are unique to mine, and even the way they dress is unfamiliar. When I observe how (and who) they worship, I get nervous. Can I ever win them to You when they seem content in their own belief system? And yet, Your Word says that I'm to preach the Gospel to all the world. I don't know how far beyond my own borders I'll ever be able to travel, but one way I can impact the lives of people around the globe is by praying. Today I choose to pray that people of all nations will be won to You, Lord. May the whole earth praise the Name of Jesus. Amen.

BE THE CHANGE
Commit to pray daily for people of every tribe, nation, and tongue.

Abiding in Him

*"If you abide in me, and my words abide in you,
ask whatever you wish, and it will be done for you."*
JOHN 15:7 ESV

Lord, I know one of the keys to receiving answers to my prayers lies in sticking close to You. I want to abide in You, Father. I want to spend time in Your presence, getting to know Your heart, Your will, Your plans for my life. When I am intent on having this very special relationship with You, it's easier to know how to pray. It's also easier to believe You will move on my behalf when I pray, because I know Your heart for me is good and not bad. So today I ask in faith for provision, for healing, and for a bright future—confident in the result because I have chosen to abide in You. I praise You, Father. Amen.

BE THE CHANGE

Offer to help decorate a friend or loved one's house.

Praying for Miracles

He replied, "If you have faith as small as a mustard seed, you can say to this mulberry tree, 'Be uprooted and planted in the sea,' and it will obey you."
LUKE 17:6 NIV

Oh how I love this biblical promise, Lord! Sometimes my faith really is as small as a mustard seed—a teensy tiny drop is all I can muster. But Your Word says that is enough. With just a drop of faith, I can look at deeply rooted issues (trees, if you will) and command them to go. Fear, be gone! Doubt, be erased! Worry, you have to go. Anger, get lost! All of these and more flee at the Name of Jesus. So today I pull out my mustard-seed faith. I square off with whatever troubles the enemy has placed in front of me and say, "Get out of here!" and I watch those trees take a flying leap. Amen.

BE THE CHANGE
*Offer your babysitting services
to a parent with little ones.*

The Spirit's Intercession

*The Spirit helps us in our weakness. For we do not know
what to pray for as we ought, but the Spirit himself
intercedes for us with groanings too deep for words.*
ROMANS 8:26 ESV

There have been many times when I didn't know how
to pray, Lord. The day my loved one died. The moment I felt overwhelming fear. That time I wondered
if I would have enough food in the house to feed my
kids. During those times, when doubt reared its head,
Your Spirit began to intercede through me, uttering
thoughts so deep, so intense, that I knew the words
could not be my own. You know just what to say, even
when I don't. You know just what to do when actions
elude me. You know just how to stand, even when I
feel like crumbling to the ground. You're my everything, Lord, and I'm so grateful to You. Amen.

BE THE CHANGE
*Use your words for good. Send letters of
appreciation to men and women in the military.*

A Prayer to Face Your Enemies

Be brave when you face your enemies. Your courage will show them that they are going to be destroyed, and it will show you that you will be saved. God will make all of this happen.
PHILIPPIANS 1:28 CEV

Sometimes I feel like such a coward, Lord. I'm not a fan of confrontation. I would rather crawl into a hole than come up against an enemy. But You're teaching me to be brave. You give me the courage I need to stand up to bullies and make an impact—all through the power of Your love. I'm also learning to pray for those who hurt me (even though it's not easy). When I take the time to do this, everything changes. I begin to see them through Your eyes, Lord, and that's the best possible perspective. Thanks for giving me courage, Father. Amen.

BE THE CHANGE
Commit to pray for those who have hurt you.

All Good Things

*We keep on praying for you, asking our God to enable you
to live a life worthy of his call. May he give you the power to
accomplish all the good things your faith prompts you to do.*
2 Thessalonians 1:11 NLT

You've got a lot for me to do, Father. I sense it. There
are big things on the horizon. Sometimes I wonder
how I'll find the time or energy to accomplish it all.
Then I'm reminded of all You've brought me through
already. I know, with Your help, I can do anything.
Today, I commit myself to pray over the things that
are coming, the things I cannot yet see. Prayer will
activate my faith and give me courage to step out
when the time comes. I know You'll give me the power
I need to accomplish *all* the good things You've placed
in my heart, but that power is birthed on my knees.
May my life be worthy of the call. Amen.

Be the Change
Keep a written list of all the ideas God is giving you.

In Secret

*"When you pray, go into your room and shut
the door and pray to your Father who is in secret.
And your Father who sees in secret will reward you."*
MATTHEW 6:6 ESV

I don't want to be the sort of person who comes
across as holier-than-thou, Lord. I don't want to stand
on the street corner telling everyone what a fine
Christian I am. Truth be told, I feel like I miss the mark
almost as many times as I hit it. That's why I love hanging out with You. You meet me in the secret places:
my bed, my favorite chair, the backyard, a nearby park.
You long to spend quiet, reflective time with me. No
jumping up and down. No shouts of celebration. Just
pure, quiet, secret time where I pour out my heart, and
You wrap Your loving arms around me and whisper,
"Peace, be still! It's going to be all right." Oh how I love
our quiet times together, Father. Amen.

BE THE CHANGE
*Choose a favorite "prayer chair"
where you can meet daily with God.*

Great, Unsearchable Things

*"Call to me and I will answer you and tell you
great and unsearchable things you do not know."*
JEREMIAH 33:3 NIV

Sometimes I feel like a know-it-all, Lord. I guess I want
to prove my worth to people by puffing myself up. But
You know better. All I am, all I have, all I will ever be is
because of You. I can only accomplish what You place
in my heart and life to accomplish. Big or small, every
task is God-ordained. I know You're preparing things
for my life journey, even now, that would blow me
away if I knew the depth of them. All I can do is trust
that You will equip me to do the work once the tasks
arrive. I know You wouldn't call me if You didn't plan
to equip me, and knowing that brings courage and
confidence. My walk with You is such an adventure,
Lord! Amen.

BE THE CHANGE
*Write down where you've come from and all of
the ways God has used you—so you'll never forget.*

The Spirit Is Willing

*"Watch and pray that you may not enter into temptation.
The spirit indeed is willing, but the flesh is weak."*
MATTHEW 26:41 ESV

I have to be on my guard at all times, Lord. Just
about the time I think my faith is stronger than ever,
temptation rears its head, and I fall right into the
enemy's trap. Ugh! These moments make me feel
like such a spiritual loser. Thankfully, You give me a
pat on the back and encourage me to keep going.
Otherwise, I might just give up. I lean heavily on You
after I take a tumble, Father. My spirit is willing to go
wherever You call, but my flesh is weaker than I'm
willing to admit. So I'll keep watching. I'll keep praying with eyes wide open so that the enemy won't get
his foot in the door. Amen.

BE THE CHANGE
Host a sock (or shoe) drive for the local homeless shelter.

Living the Gospel

*I appeal to you therefore, brothers, by the mercies of
God, to present your bodies as a living sacrifice, holy
and acceptable to God, which is your spiritual worship.*
ROMANS 12:1 ESV

Father, I confess the words *living sacrifice* used to make
me nervous. I pictured myself on the foreign mission
field, surrounded by cannibals, ready to offer my life
in service to the Gospel. I see now that presenting
myself as a living sacrifice simply means I'm willing
to get uncomfortable, should the need arise. I'll get
up earlier to pray. I'll speak to someone who hasn't
been particularly nice to me. I'll go out of my way to
care for those in need. I'll put others ahead of myself
(something that definitely doesn't come naturally). I
can't do any of these things without Your help, Lord,
so feel free to embolden me as only You can. I praise
You for using me. Amen.

BE THE CHANGE

*Get out of your comfort zone! Host a
small group or Bible study in your home.*

Loving Your Enemies

*"I tell you, love your enemies and
pray for those who persecute you."*
MATTHEW 5:44 NIV

This is a tough one, Lord. I'm more inclined to talk
badly about my enemies or seek revenge for the
things they've done to hurt me than to love them.
But I know Your ways are higher than my own. You're
teaching me how to impact the world for the Gospel,
and that includes praying for my enemies. So I'll pray
for those who've talked about me behind my back.
For those who've ridiculed the way I look. For those
who roll their eyes when I start talking about my faith.
For those across the globe who hate the convictions
of Christians. For those who lash out at believers on
social media. You want me to pray for everyone—the
good, the bad, and the ugly. Today I commit to do that.
I will start with those who have wounded me personally
and go from there. Help me, I pray. Amen.

BE THE CHANGE

*Be a positive voice on social media. Instead of bantering and
stirring up negativity, post positive, uplifting messages.*

Heart, Soul, and Mind

*Trust in the LORD with all your heart, and do not lean
on your own understanding. In all your ways acknowledge
him, and he will make straight your paths.*
PROVERBS 3:5–6 ESV

It's not enough that I love You with my heart, Lord.
I have to love You with my mind and my soul—my
thoughts, my wishes, and my dreams must all align
with You. I will love You with my goals, my aspirations,
my tomorrows. To truly love You means I have to trust
that You're for me not against me. I have to believe
that loving You is the answer to any problem, any trial
I might face. In loving You I find rest. I find comfort.
I find peace. I find solutions. You're truly my be-all
and end-all, Father. There is none like You, and I'm so
grateful to be Your child. Amen.

BE THE CHANGE
*Make a list of all your hopes, wishes, and dreams,
and then attempt to see them through God's eyes.*

That You May Proclaim

You are a chosen race, a royal priesthood, a holy nation, a people for his own possession, that you may proclaim the excellencies of him who called you out of darkness into his marvelous light.
1 PETER 2:9 ESV

You didn't choose me so that I could sit on the sofa and revel in Your love (though I enjoy doing that, of course). You chose me, You called me, You gave me Your Name so that I could impact lives. Your aim wasn't just to make Your kids feel special and included but to empower them to proclaim Your excellencies to the nations! We impact lives when we open up and share our stories of how You delivered us out of darkness. Our testimonies change people and touch nations. There's power in speaking up! So give me the courage to do that today, I pray. Amen.

BE THE CHANGE
Encourage everyone in your inner circle to write down and share how God has delivered them out of darkness into His marvelous light.

Until That Day

*I pray that your love will keep on growing and that you will
fully know and understand how to make the right choices.
Then you will still be pure and innocent when Christ returns.
And until that day, Jesus Christ will keep you busy doing
good deeds that bring glory and praise to God.*

PHILIPPIANS 1:9–11 CEV

Lord, You're showing me day by day how to make better choices. I can see growth in my spiritual life, and I'm grateful for it. I'm finally figuring out how to say no to the bad stuff and yes to the good. I want, more than anything, to please You. One of the reasons I'm so intent on this is because I know people are watching. They know I'm a Christian, and they're curious to see if I am actually as dedicated to my beliefs as I say I am. I want to be authentic, the real deal. I never want to be called a hypocrite. You've cleansed me with Your blood. May I live a life worthy of that cleansing—one filled with good deeds that bring glory to Your Name. Amen.

BE THE CHANGE
Offer to shovel a neighbor's sidewalk.

A Hearty Life

Whatever you do, work heartily, as for the Lord and not for men, knowing that from the Lord you will receive the inheritance as your reward. You are serving the Lord Christ.
COLOSSIANS 3:23–24 ESV

I'm not always a "hearty" worker, Lord. Sometimes I don't give it my best. I slink off into the shadows and hope that others will take up the slack. I'm low on energy. I don't have the "want to." But You're teaching me that serving You means I have to get with the program. You'll provide the necessary energy through Your Holy Spirit to get the tasks done. And what admirable tasks they are, Father! You want me to reach this world for You by living a worthy life. So I commit to work heartily, keeping those who don't yet know You in mind. I'm working for You, after all, and I'm a servant who is humbled to be called. Amen.

BE THE CHANGE
Ship a care package to a ministry or individual.

The Power to Bring Salvation

*I am not ashamed of the gospel, because it is the
power of God that brings salvation to everyone
who believes: first to the Jew, then to the Gentile.*
ROMANS 1:16 NIV

I'm not ashamed, Lord—not ashamed of the Gospel, not ashamed of the life You've called me to, not ashamed to make Your Name known throughout this earth. No hiding under a bushel for me! I'll proclaim Your good works to all who will listen. This proclamation of the Gospel message carries with it the power to bring salvation. Wow! People can be saved if I speak up. You've swung wide the doors, Lord. With twenty-first-century advances, my words can go far. So, give me creative ideas to know where and when to speak up. I can't wait to get started! Amen.

BE THE CHANGE

*Start a blog where friends and family members
can share their testimonies. That way, people from
around the globe can read and be impacted.*

The Narrow Gate

"Enter by the narrow gate. For the gate is wide and the way is easy that leads to destruction, and those who enter by it are many. For the gate is narrow and the way is hard that leads to life, and those who find it are few."
MATTHEW 7:13–14 ESV

The Gospel message flies in the face of political correctness, Lord. The world would have me believe that all roads lead to heaven and that all people are right, no matter what they believe. It's getting to the point where it's hard to speak out or stand up for my faith for fear that others will label me as bigoted or cruel. I'm neither, Lord! I love all people. But I have to face facts—there's only one way to heaven and that's through Your Son, Jesus Christ. I'll go on proclaiming that message, no matter how difficult, because it's the truth. It's also a message that will change lives, which is my goal (and Yours as well). Help me as I speak up, I pray. Amen.

BE THE CHANGE
Speak the truth in love.

Doing Good

Do not forget to do good and to share with others,
for with such sacrifices God is pleased.
HEBREWS 13:16 NIV

I've heard the phrase *do-gooder* all my life, Lord. I'm
not sure I would consider myself a do-gooder, but
the idea holds some appeal! I'd like to be known as
someone who's generous to others, who cares more
about the needs of those around me than personal
wants and wishes. So don't let me forget! Keep me
tuned in to those who are hurting—in my neighborhood, my church, my workplace. I don't want to be
guilty of marching right past someone in need without
stopping to pray, offer aid, and uplift. I know You care
deeply about those in need, Father, so increase my
awareness and give me Your heart for hurting human-
ity. Amen.

BE THE CHANGE
Send a "just because" card to a coworker
who's going through a rough patch.

No Other Name

*"There is salvation in no one else, for
there is no other name under heaven given
among men by which we must be saved."*
ACTS 4:12 ESV

There's so much power in the Name of Jesus! Oh how I love to speak that Name. When I'm up against the greatest foe—"Jesus!" When I'm in need of healing—"Jesus!" When everything seems to be going against me, the Name of Jesus brings immediate calm. No wonder the enemy is so intent on squelching Jesus' Name. It brings power, gives life, and radiates joy. Today, I choose to speak that Name with full abandon, for there truly is no other Name by which mankind will be saved. I praise You, Jesus! Amen.

BE THE CHANGE
*Lay down your fears and concerns and
speak the Name of Jesus with boldness!*

Sworn Friendship

Jonathan said to David, "Go in peace, for we have sworn friendship with each other in the name of the LORD, saying, 'The LORD is witness between you and me, and between your descendants and my descendants forever.'" Then David left, and Jonathan went back to the town.
1 SAMUEL 20:42 NIV

There are those friendships, Lord, that are meant to last forever. I don't have a lot of "forever" friends, but a few will be with me for the rest of my life. I know that circumstances might change. I know that time and space might catch us off guard. But for now, I'm in for the long haul with my forever friends. They've impacted my life and changed me in so many ways. I hope the same can be said in reverse. When it comes to changing the world, I plan to do it one friend at a time. And I guess this would be a good time to mention that You're my very best friend. I'm sticking with You till the very end. Amen.

BE THE CHANGE
Offer to babysit a friend's kiddos.

Encouraged, Built Up

*Therefore encourage one another and build
one another up, just as you are doing.*
1 THESSALONIANS 5:11 ESV

I've had friendships that drained me and friendships that charged my batteries. I'll stick with the positive ones, Lord. Your idea of the perfect friendship for me is one that builds me up not one that tears me down. I've had plenty of friends who wanted to plunge me down to their level. No thanks! Point me in the direction of godly people who will help me to grow in my relationship with You. And let me just say that You're the most encouraging friend I've got! If I ever need cheering up, I just open Your love letter to me and start reading. The Bible is filled—cover to cover—with encouraging words. Thanks for that, Lord. Amen.

BE THE CHANGE
*Offer to put together furniture for
a single mom or person in need.*

Forgiving Friendship

*Make allowance for each other's faults,
and forgive anyone who offends you. Remember,
the Lord forgave you, so you must forgive others.*
COLOSSIANS 3:13 NLT

My feelings were hurt recently, Lord. It's happened before, but this time it really stung. I know what Your Word says: I need to forgive when someone hurts me. But I'm not altogether sure it won't happen again. Okay, I know I've done things that need forgiving too. I'm not a perfect friend either. Help us to figure this out, please. Show us how to guard our tongues and how to make allowance for each other's faults. I want to be quick to forgive in part because I'm hoping people will be quick to forgive me when I mess up. I can't help but think about the many times You've had to forgive me, after all. You've shown me by example what a true friendship looks like. I'm so grateful. Amen.

BE THE CHANGE
Offer to take a sick friend's kids to school.

Closer Than a Brother

A man of many companions may come to ruin,
but there is a friend who sticks closer than a brother.
PROVERBS 18:24 ESV

I've had a handful of "closer than a brother" friends in
my life, Lord, and I cherish them. It's hard to imagine
that anyone could be closer than a sibling, but I've
experienced this kind of relationship firsthand. When
I form a bond that tight, it's a real gift. We're on the
same wavelength. We each know what the other is
thinking and what responses to expect during life's
ups and downs. Best of all, I know for a fact that
these friends aren't going anywhere, even if I mess
up. They've got a real stick-to-it attitude and won't
give up on me. I won't give up on them either. They're
worth the effort, Lord. Thanks for bringing them into
my life. Amen.

BE THE CHANGE
Surprise your BFF with an unexpected, well-thought-out gift.

Iron-Sharpening Friendships

As iron sharpens iron,
so one person sharpens another.
PROVERBS 27:17 NIV

My friend makes me better, Lord. Like iron sharpening iron, this amazing friend smooths off my rough edges and makes me a greater human being. This is someone who is good at speaking truth (and has even hurt my feelings a time or two because of it) and who counters these remarks with amazing love and kindness. I need someone like this—someone who wants to make me better, someone who I adore. Show me how to sharpen in return. Not in a hurtful way, of course, but in love—as has been done for me. Together, we'll grow stronger and stronger each day. Amen.

BE THE CHANGE
Offer to run errands for a friend with a busy schedule.

Earnest Counsel

*Oil and perfume make the heart glad, and the
sweetness of a friend comes from his earnest counsel.*
PROVERBS 27:9 ESV

Sometimes I just need a friend who makes the time
for me. It seems like most people are so busy rushing
from place to place no one has time to sit over a cup
of coffee and share a good, long chat. But that's what
I long for—a friend who takes the time, even when
it's a bit of a sacrifice. For only in spending quality
time together can bonding take place. There, in those
quiet friend-to-friend moments, I can both give and
receive earnest counsel, bathed in love. No rush. No
judgment. No manipulation. Just pure, godly counsel,
straight from the heart of one who really cares about
me. Thank You for friends who take the time to share,
Lord. Amen.

BE THE CHANGE
Offer to clean your friend's car, inside and out.

Two Are Better Than One

*Two are better than one, because they
have a good return for their labor.*
ECCLESIASTES 4:9 NIV

I remember that old expression, Lord: many hands
make light work. I know it's true. When I've got a big
task (cleaning out the garage, redecorating a room,
baking for a crowd), I call on a friend to join me. My
friend keeps me laughing and chatting as we work, and
we get a lot done too! I know that two are better than
one when it comes to prayer as well. If one can put a
thousand enemies to flight, two can put ten thousand!
That's why I call on godly friends to pray with me when
I'm really going through the muck, because I know
the impact they will make with their prayers. Thanks
so much for blessing me with the kind of friends who
lighten my load, Father. May I be that kind of friend in
return. Amen.

BE THE CHANGE
Help a good friend host a party.

Walking with the Wise

Walk with the wise and become wise,
for a companion of fools suffers harm.
PROVERBS 13:20 NIV

We become like the ones we hang out with. I know that's true, Lord. I've seen it in my own life. When I hang out with people who are lazy or slothful, I become more like that myself. When I hang out with people who see the benefit of hard work, I'm more prone to work hard. It's easy to see that we rub off on each other! Point me in the direction of those who will be good influences in my life. And make me a good influence as well. I don't want to rub off on people in the wrong way—by gossiping about others, wasting time, or giving in to temptation. May I learn from the wise and give off wisdom in return. Amen.

BE THE CHANGE
Help a friend on moving day.

God's Intimate Friendship

"Oh, for the days when I was in my prime,
when God's intimate friendship blessed my house."
JOB 29:4 NIV

I have plenty of intimate friends, Lord—the kind I can share my heart with. These friends know when I'm going through a hard time (emotionally, financially, or otherwise). They know when I'm struggling with temptation or headed off in the wrong direction with another relationship. I love these intimate friends. But You know who I love even more, Lord? You! You don't just know me. You know me from the inside out. You know what makes me tick, why I behave the way I do, what my heart truly longs for. You're the most precious friend of all because You cared enough to die in my place so that I could live forever. How can any friend ever top that? Oh how I adore You, Lord! Amen.

BE THE CHANGE
Use your talents to bless someone.

Praying for Your Friends

After Job had prayed for his friends,
the LORD restored his fortunes and gave
him twice as much as he had before.
JOB 42:10 NIV

There are so many lessons to be learned from Job's story, Lord, but here's one I almost overlooked: You waited to restore Job's fortune until after he had prayed for his friends. Sometimes I wonder why You're taking so long to move on my behalf. Maybe You're just waiting on me! Maybe it's time for me to lift up a prayer so that You're free to move. I hadn't thought about that before. I want to be someone who lifts up others in prayer not just during rough seasons but on a regular basis. Thanks for the reminder that praying for them is both a blessing and an honor. Amen.

BE THE CHANGE
Make a list of friends who need prayer
right now. Then start praying!

The Gates of Hell Will Not Prevail

"I tell you, you are Peter, and on this rock I will build my church, and the gates of hell shall not prevail against it."
MATTHEW 16:18 ESV

Is there anything finer than spending time in the house of God with fellow believers? Nothing quite matches the feelings of joy and camaraderie that envelop me when I'm surrounded on every side by people who are lifting up Your Name in praise. As we sing, as we worship, as we listen to Your Word, we're invigorated. We grow together, learn together, share together, pray together. All of it, together. And the gates of hell won't prevail against us, not as long as we live in unity with one another. What a powerhouse we are when we come together in Your Name, Lord. Amen!

BE THE CHANGE
Offer to help in the church nursery.

Keeping Watch Over the Flock

"Keep watch over yourselves and all the flock of which the Holy Spirit has made you overseers. Be shepherds of the church of God, which he bought with his own blood."
ACTS 20:28 NIV

I want to be a friend to those in need, especially inside my own church, Lord. Help me to keep my eyes opened and my ears tuned in so that I don't overlook anyone who might be hurting. Give me creative ideas to care for the ones who need extra TLC—the shut-ins, the sick, the ones struggling financially, the single moms. I want to make myself accessible to those who need a friend so that no one walks alone. I'm so grateful for the many times You've surrounded me with fellow believers during my low seasons, Father. Now I want to uplift others as I've been uplifted. Show me how, I pray. Amen.

BE THE CHANGE
Volunteer at your church.

Meeting Together

Let us consider how to stir up one another to love and good works, not neglecting to meet together, as is the habit of some, but encouraging one another, and all the more as you see the Day drawing near.
HEBREWS 10:24–25 ESV

It's easy to get out of the habit, Lord. Some Sundays I just don't feel like getting out of bed or making the drive. But You've shown me, time and time again, how different my day can be when I make the effort to go to church even when I don't feel like it. So continue giving me those nudges, Lord. Don't let me slip into laziness or apathy. Keep me yearning for time with You and with my fellow believers. I want to go on stirring others up to good works, and that can only happen when we're actually together. This is more important now than ever, since the day of Christ's return is drawing closer. Bind us together, Lord, I pray. Amen.

BE THE CHANGE
Give someone at church a big hug.

Two or Three

*"Where two or three gather in my name,
there am I with them."*
MATTHEW 18:20 NIV

A church congregation doesn't have to be huge to make a big impact, does it, Lord? Your Word says that even two or three—when they link their hearts, minds, and prayers—can change the world. This is why the body of Christ is so important. We weren't meant to walk this road alone, were we? I've learned the benefits of sticking with a tight-knit group of fellow believers. There's amazing power when we walk, talk, and pray in unity. You've taught me that You're with us when we gather together, Lord. What an amazing promise to have You in our midst! Oh how we need You! Amen.

BE THE CHANGE

*Offer to host a Sunday brunch for singles.
Pray for the needs of those in attendance.*

Gifts to Build the Church

*What then, brothers? When you come together, each
one has a hymn, a lesson, a revelation, a tongue, or an
interpretation. Let all things be done for building up.*
1 CORINTHIANS 14:26 ESV

I love how You work, Lord! You give different gifts to
different members of the body of Christ. One person
sings. Another teaches. Another has the gift of hospi-
tality and loves to serve as a greeter. Some enjoy praying with the sick. Still others love preparing meals for
women's events or men's breakfasts. There's (literally)
a slot for everyone to fill. From finances to janitorial
duties, there's work to be done in the local church.
Thanks for showing us that we each can play a role. I'll
never feel left out as long as we work together.
(Thanks for including me!) Amen.

BE THE CHANGE
Offer to teach a class at your church.

Equipped

*And [Christ] gave the apostles, the prophets, the evangelists,
the shepherds and teachers, to equip the saints for the
work of ministry, for building up the body of Christ.*
EPHESIANS 4:11–12 ESV

I would expect to be on a learning curve when starting a new job, Lord, so I'm not sure why I would feel differently about my role at church. It takes a while to settle in and for me to discover my spiritual gifts. Will I teach? Sing in the choir? Help in the church office? Print newsletters? Help out with the church's website? There are so many areas where I might fit in, but I'm not sure which one is right yet. What I do know is, even now, You're equipping me to be of benefit to my local church body. I can hardly wait to see where I'll end up, Lord, but I trust You with the process. Amen.

BE THE CHANGE
Stuff envelopes in the church office.

By One Spirit

We were all baptized by one Spirit so as to form
one body—whether Jews or Gentiles, slave or free—
and we were all given the one Spirit to drink.
1 CORINTHIANS 12:13 NIV

There's so much disunity in the world today, Lord. It's almost like people are working overtime to put up walls of separation. May that never be the case inside the body of Christ. We are, after all, baptized by one Spirit—Your Holy Spirit. No matter where we came from, no matter our color or heritage, if we are truly Christians, then we are one in You. You've unified us, stitched us together into a colorful quilt known as the body of Christ. That quilt wouldn't be as beautiful if we were all cut from the same cloth. May our differences never separate us, Lord. May they only draw us closer, I pray. Amen.

BE THE CHANGE
Celebrate your pastor during
Pastor Appreciation Month.

I Was Glad

I was glad when they said to me,
"Let us go to the house of the LORD!"
PSALM 122:1 ESV

There are so many things I get excited about, Lord—
ball games, family reunions, parties, celebrations,
holidays, banquets. As I count down the days, my ex-
citement builds. I can hardly wait! That's also how I feel
about going to church on Sundays. With each weekday
that passes, my heart cries out, "It's coming! Another
opportunity to worship the One I love with those I
love." As I look at today's scripture, I'm reminded that,
even thousands of years ago, King David was amped
up over going to the house of the Lord. Not much has
changed, has it? There's something so special about
spending time in corporate worship after all. Amen.

BE THE CHANGE
Offer to carpool new believers to church.

All Things

*God placed all things under his feet and appointed him to
be head over everything for the church, which is his body,
the fullness of him who fills everything in every way.*
EPHESIANS 1:22–23 NIV

Lord, I love that Your Word makes it clear that all
things are placed under the feet of Your Son, Jesus.
He's the head of the church, the King of my life, and
the only Savior I will ever need. I can place all things
under His control—my heart, my thoughts, my mistakes, my pain, my sickness. He cares about it all and
longs for me to rest in Him. Today I choose to do just
that. I won't wait until I'm sitting in church on Sunday
morning. Right here, right now, I'll give Him my heart-
aches, my bitterness, my struggles. Take them, I pray,
and release me from any burdens attached to them.
I'm so grateful I can trust You in *all* things, Lord. Amen.

BE THE CHANGE
Visit church members who are sick or in the hospital.

Commitments to the Lord

When they had appointed elders for them in every church, with prayer and fasting they committed them to the Lord in whom they had believed.
ACTS 14:23 ESV

Oh how I love this image, Lord! When men and women are called into service for You, the whole body has a role to play. You've instructed church members to gather around them, to pray and fast, and then to send them out to do Your work. This act of committing people to service is precious. It's a reminder to those who are sent that they are not alone. It also reminds those who stay behind to remain diligent in prayer for the duration of their brothers' and sisters' work. I'm so grateful to all who've responded to Your call, Lord. May I always remember them in prayer, no matter where their ministry takes them. Amen.

BE THE CHANGE
Put the photo of someone who has been called into ministry on your refrigerator, where you can see it and pray daily.

Changing

Your wife will be like a fruitful vine within your house;
your children will be like olive shoots around your table.
PSALM 128:3 NIV

Lord, I'm so blessed to have my family. When I look around at all of the loved ones who make up my world, I consider it pure joy. Mothers, fathers, siblings, children, aunts, uncles, cousins, and close friends who might as well be family—I love them all. I think it's wonderful that You've given me this tight-knit group to love. May I always impact each person for good, especially the little ones. May no one ever turn away from You because of my actions or behavior. If I can change my family—turn their hearts toward You—then I can change the world. My family members will go on to impact others who will impact others. A long chain of events can take place, and I can play a role. How amazing, Lord! Amen.

BE THE CHANGE
Offer to work out with a family
member who wants to get in shape.

Training Up a Child

Train up a child in the way he should go;
even when he is old he will not depart from it.
PROVERBS 22:6 ESV

I've studied this verse for a while now, Lord. When You give me children to raise or mentor, I know You've given me a holy task. If I do all that I can to train up these children in the way they should go—teaching them Your Word, Your precepts, Your heart—then I affect eternity. I love this promise that a child who's been trained in Your ways will never depart from You. I'm claiming that promise for all of the children in my world, Lord. May I never be a hindrance. May I always be a positive, uplifting trainer—one who shows these kiddos what the heart of God looks like. Amen.

BE THE CHANGE
Offer to host a children's Bible study group in your home.

One Father

For this reason I bow my knees before the Father,
from whom every family in heaven and on earth is named.
EPHESIANS 3:14–15 ESV

Lord, it's amazing to think that I'm connected to every single family on planet earth through You, my heavenly Father. I have brothers and sisters I'll never meet in this life, but we'll get to know each other in heaven. Those of us who have come to saving grace in Jesus all bow our knees to You, our Lord, our Healer, our Deliverer, our gracious Father. No matter what language we speak, how we dress, what foods we eat, or the color of our skin, our spiritual DNA is linked through You, Lord! How can we ever thank You adequately for including all of us in Your family? What a blessing that You love and are loved by so many of Your kids. Amen.

BE THE CHANGE
Become a pen pal with a fellow
believer in a different country.

As Christ Loved the Church

*Husbands, love your wives, just as Christ
loved the church and gave himself up for her.*
EPHESIANS 5:25 NIV

Lord, I can't even fathom how much Your Son loves
us—His bride. His affection is so deep that He was willing to lay down His life for us. This sacrificial love goes
beyond anything I've ever witnessed in the natural.
I know no one willing to give like this. And yet we're
instructed to show that sort of love to those within
our own families. What a difference it would make if
we offered sacrificial love to husbands, wives, children,
siblings, aunts, uncles, and cousins. We could impact
so many in our inner circle. Then they, likewise, could
influence others in their circles. We could change the
world with this sort of love, Lord. Help us to display it
for all to see. Amen.

BE THE CHANGE
Offer to do someone else's chores.

A Long and Happy Life

*Children, you belong to the Lord, and you do the right
thing when you obey your parents. The first commandment
with a promise says, "Obey your father and your mother,
and you will have a long and happy life."*
EPHESIANS 6:1–3 CEV

I wish I had understood this verse as a child, Lord. Back
then, I didn't realize that obeying my parents would
lead to a long and happy life. But I get it now. I'm keen
on making sure the children in my world understand
it too, so that they can live long and prosperous lives.
This is the first commandment with a promise, as Your
Word says, but that doesn't mean obedience comes
naturally. Some of the children I know find it more difficult to be obedient than others. But You can manage
even the unruliest child. I ask You to do that for the
well-being of my family. Amen.

BE THE CHANGE
Offer to tutor a child who is struggling in school.

You and Your Household

They said, "Believe in the Lord Jesus, and you will be saved, you and your household." And they spoke the word of the Lord to him and to all who were in his house. And he took them the same hour of the night and washed their wounds; and he was baptized at once, he and all his family. Then he brought them up into his house and set food before them. And he rejoiced along with his entire household that he had believed in God.
Acts 16:31–34 esv

Father, thank You for including my household. You didn't just want my heart, You wanted the hearts of everyone I hold dear—family members from the oldest to the youngest. I pray for all of them, that they would walk with You all the days of their lives. May they serve You with joy and thanksgiving in their hearts. How happy I am to know that You loved us all so much that You swept us into the fold. Amen.

Be the Change
Trace your family's lineage and save it for future generations.

You Are My People

Say to your brothers, "You are my people,"
and to your sisters, "You have received mercy."
HOSEA 2:1 ESV

It's a wonderful feeling, Lord, to be completely bonded with family members. To be on the same wavelength. To live in harmony. I can look them in the eye and say, "You're my people!" (Hopefully, they feel the same way about me.) I feel a family atmosphere when I'm hanging out with my brothers and sisters in Christ too. We really are one big happy family, joined together by our faith. I wouldn't want it any other way, Lord. Thank You for blessing me with so many people to love. Amen.

BE THE CHANGE
Offer to mow a sick or elderly neighbor's yard.

Caring for the Elderly in Our Families

*For the sake of my family and friends,
I will say, "Peace be within you."*
PSALM 122:8 NIV

Lord, this one is near and dear to my heart. Today I
want to pay homage to the elderly in my family—the
grandparents, elderly parents, aunts, uncles, and so
on. What amazing role models they are! They have
changed lives for the better. I've learned so much
about how to live from those who've walked before
(those who are still with us and those who have already
passed on). Show me how to honor those in their
golden years, to treat them with dignity and respect.
Help me to care for the ones in need with the tender-
ness they showed me as a small child. I want to bless
them and You, Lord. Help me, I pray. Amen.

BE THE CHANGE
*Plan an outing or a special event
for someone in their golden years.*

Especially Those in the Family of Believers

Therefore, as we have opportunity, let us do good to all people,
especially to those who belong to the family of believers.
GALATIANS 6:10 NIV

I know we're called to treat all people with love and
respect, Lord, but I'm glad You gave us a little nudge in
this verse to be especially good to those in the body
of Christ. I have such admiration for my spiritual
brothers and sisters. Many have lived difficult lives,
but they have persevered for the sake of the Gospel.
I can't help but admire them. Show me how to bring
honor to the ones who've been so good to me and my
family. I want to bless them for their years of service
and love. Give me fun and creative ideas so that I can
bring honor where honor is due, Lord. Amen.

BE THE CHANGE
Spend an afternoon making homemade
ice cream with other believers.

Obedience

He must manage his own family well and see that his children obey him, and he must do so in a manner worthy of full respect.
1 TIMOTHY 3:4 NIV

This is a tough one, Lord. It's not always easy to get little ones (or even big ones) to obey. Sometimes I get a little frazzled in my attempts. Then I remember how patient You've been with me, how many times You've had to adjust my attitude over the years. I'm so grateful for Your tender, loving care, Father. May I be just as caring with those You've placed in my charge—whether they be children, grandchildren, students, or kiddos in the neighborhood. I don't want to be lenient to a fault, but neither do I want to break any tender spirits. Show me how to bring balance, that I might lead by example. Thank You, Lord. Amen.

BE THE CHANGE
Offer to do a loved one's laundry or help with homework.

Speaking in Faith

*Faith is confidence in what we hope for
and assurance about what we do not see.
This is what the ancients were commended for.*
HEBREWS 11:1–2 NIV

Faith. What a marvelous word! Faith gives me the courage to step out and do what only a few moments ago felt impossible. When I learn to speak in faith, I am emboldened. I feel courageous. I can pray in faith, believing for miracles. I can walk with expectation, ready to see the hand of God in my everyday life. Faith gives me confidence in the (yet) unseen—it makes me sure of things that haven't happened yet. I can pray for the sick, believe financial provision is on the way, and hope for the best possible outcomes. I want to be like the men and women in the Bible who were commended for their great faith, Lord. I'm already on my way. I can't wait to witness Your great and mighty acts as I stand in faith and believe. Amen.

BE THE CHANGE
*Offer to pray for your restaurant server,
and then leave a generous tip.*

If You Have Faith

*"Whatever you ask in prayer,
you will receive, if you have faith."*
MATTHEW 21:22 ESV

If. What a tiny little word, and yet how powerful. I
can have whatever I ask for in prayer, Lord, if I have
faith. There have been times I've asked for frivolous
things (and I'm glad You didn't say yes to all of my
silly requests as a child). But when it comes to the
big stuff—praying for those in need, pleading on
behalf of a friend in a troubled marriage or a loved
one with cancer—I want my "if" to be as solid as a rock.
Strengthen my faith so that I can believe in the miraculous. I want to see Your hand at work in supernatural
ways. I want to witness lives changed, marriages
impacted, relationships restored. I want to come into
my prayer closet with such a steady faith that I walk
out ready to witness miracles firsthand. I can't wait to
see how You move, Lord! Amen.

BE THE CHANGE
Offer to disciple new believers.

Increasing Our Faith

The apostles said to the Lord, "Increase our faith!"
LUKE 17:5 NIV

So many things have increased as I've gotten older, Lord: My waistline. My income. The size of my home, my family. Even my church is bigger! But there's one area of my life where I truly want to see increase, Lord, and that's in my faith. Take my mustard seed of faith and blossom it into a whole tree, I pray. Stretch it. Grow it. Multiply it. May it be like a wildfire, out of control, ready to consume my life. I want to experience all that You have to offer, Lord, so do an amazing work in my heart and spirit, I pray. Amen.

BE THE CHANGE
Commit to regular monthly support of a favorite local ministry or outreach organization.

The Word Goes Forth

"So shall my word be that goes out from my mouth; it shall not return to me empty, but it shall accomplish that which I purpose, and shall succeed in the thing for which I sent it."
ISAIAH 55:11 ESV

There's power in Your Word, Lord! This I've learned firsthand. When I speak the words from the Bible aloud, I'm speaking Your heart, Your will, Your love. Those words reverberate over dire circumstances and situations, but never return void. If I speak peace into a situation, I can expect peace to come. If I speak healing, I believe for healing. The very purpose for which You have me send those words out is accomplished— not because of anything I've done, but because of who You are. Thank You for giving us Your Word, Lord. It is a powerful weapon in my hands, one I'm most grateful for. Amen.

BE THE CHANGE

Write down scriptures and post them around your house. Speak the words aloud as often as possible so that you can commit them to memory.

Speaking the Name

*"By faith in the name of Jesus, this man whom
you see and know was made strong. It is Jesus'
name and the faith that comes through him that
has completely healed him, as you can all see."*
ACTS 3:16 NIV

The Name of Jesus changes everything! At that Name,
nations bow. Demons flee. Situations change. Lives
are affected for eternity. The Name of Jesus is one I
love to speak, Lord! I cry out, "Jesus, come into this
situation and bring change!" or "In the Name of Jesus,
I command anger to leave!" There's power in that
Name—power to effect permanent change in the life
of someone who's addicted or in pain. Without that
Name, I don't know where I'd be. Lost, for sure! Oh,
but everything in my life has changed because of that
amazing Name. Amen.

BE THE CHANGE
*Speak the Name of Jesus over a situation
you're currently going through.*

By Faith, We Understand

*By faith we understand that the universe was
created by the word of God, so that what is seen
was not made out of things that are visible.*
HEBREWS 11:3 ESV

There are things I'll never understand, Lord—why
people give in to temptation, how a parent can abuse
a child, why a person would turn away from You and
return to a life of sin. But You're dropping the shack-
les from my eyes. I'm now able to see from a spiritual
point of view. I notice when the enemy is at work,
tempting and toying with believers. With eyes of faith,
I see and understand how it's possible to take a leap
into the unknown—both good and bad. I also see that
it's more important than ever to stick close to You
and to ask for Your perspective on things. These are
precarious times we're living in, Lord. Thank You for
giving me eyes to see what's really going on out there.
Amen.

BE THE CHANGE
Keep your spiritual eyes open.

Doubt, a Troublesome Weasel

"Truly I tell you, if anyone says to this mountain, 'Go, throw yourself into the sea,' and does not doubt in their heart but believes that what they say will happen, it will be done for them."
MARK 11:23 NIV

I'll be doing just fine, Lord, and then—*bam!* Doubt creeps in. Five minutes ago, I was a spiritual powerhouse. Now I'm cowering in the corner, wondering where my faith went. How quickly I forget the things You've done before—how You've proven Yourself time and time again. I want a renewal of faith, Lord, one so strong that no doubt can weasel its way in. I want the kind of faith that looks at obstacles as jumping-off points not giving-up points. I want to be able to look at the enemy's tactics and, with the wave of a hand, dismiss them with a few words from the Bible. Rid me of doubt, I pray, so that I can move mountains in Your Name. Amen.

BE THE CHANGE

Write the words PRAY AND DON'T DOUBT on a slip of paper and post it on your bathroom mirror.

The Power of the Tongue

Death and life are in the power of the tongue,
and those who love it will eat its fruits.
PROVERBS 18:21 ESV

I've heard it all my life, Lord—the power of life and death is in the tongue. I don't often pause to think about that phrase, but it's so true. I can take people out or lift them up with my words. I can encourage my child or bring such deep discouragement it takes years for them to wallow out of it—all with my words. With the power of my tongue, I can heal a friendship or cause a rift so deep it's irreparable. My choice today (and always) is to speak life into situations, to be known as one who shares positive thoughts, uplifting words. I don't ever want to be caught speaking ill of people or cutting them down. May this tongue only be used to speak life, I pray. Amen.

BE THE CHANGE
Brag on someone you know
who's overcome an obstacle.

Let There Be Light!

God said, "Let there be light," and there was light.
GENESIS 1:3 ESV

With just a few words, Lord, You formed earth. You split light from darkness. You created animals. You birthed humans onto the planet. You spoke, and things happened instantaneously. Nothing has changed over the years. You're the same, Lord—yesterday, today, and forever. And You're still speaking. You speak life over hopeless situations. You speak peace to troubled hearts. You speak healing to those in pain. Your words are as powerful today as ever. I know, because I've experienced them in my life. You spoke into my heart, and my life was transformed for all of eternity! I praise You for how You've spoken in the past and continue to speak. Amen.

BE THE CHANGE
*Write down three things that God
is speaking over you today.*

Calling Things into Existence

It is written, "I have made you the father of many nations"—in
the presence of the God in whom he believed, who gives life to
the dead and calls into existence the things that do not exist.
ROMANS 4:17 ESV

I love the image these words present, Father! You call
things into existence that did not exist before. That's
what happened during creation week. You spoke
all sorts of things into existence—giraffes with long
necks, woodpeckers, dogs, cats, hyenas, hooting owls,
mountains that touched the sky, raging rivers, and so
much more. I love Your imagination, Father! I want
that same kind of imagination so that when I speak life
into my situations, amazing things will spring forth.
How gracious You are to put so much power into the
spoken Word. I'm forever grateful for the ability to
speak into the darkness and see light. Amen.

BE THE CHANGE

Speak life over a particularly difficult situation today.
Ask God to increase your faith so that you
might see a miracle take place.

An Attitude of Gratitude

This is the day that the L<small>ORD</small> has made;
let us rejoice and be glad in it.
P<small>SALM</small> 118:24 <small>ESV</small>

You give me so many choices, Lord. I have the option to sit around and whine over my situations or to speak in faith over them. I can choose to see my lack or focus on the many times You've come through for me in the past. I can focus on petty, childish things or offer up an attitude of gratitude, even when I'm going through a rough patch. Your Word encourages me to remain positive even when life hits me with hard situations. I know there's power in praise, so today I choose to offer up powerful words of thanksgiving, no matter what I'm walking through. You've been so good to me, Lord. How can I help but praise Your Name? Amen.

B<small>E THE</small> C<small>HANGE</small>

Make a list of the top ten things you're thankful for,
and then praise God for every item on the list.

For He Is Good

Give thanks to the LORD, for he is good;
his love endures forever.
PSALM 107:1 NIV

You are good, Lord. If that's all I ever know about You, it's enough. You're good—to Your people, to all of creation. I can trust that Your responses will be for my good and that Your heart for me is good. I never have to wonder if You're out to get me or mad at me when I make mistakes. Your heart is always and forever on my side. There are no human beings I can say that about. Even the best people I know sometimes slip up and do bad or unexpected things. When it comes to You, however, my expectations are always the same. I can count on You, my good, good Father. Amen.

BE THE CHANGE

On your social media page, post a list
of the ways God has proven Himself good.

Unshaken

*Let us be grateful for receiving a kingdom that
cannot be shaken, and thus let us offer to God
acceptable worship, with reverence and awe.*
HEBREWS 12:28 ESV

I've been through some tough challenges, Lord, as
You know. You were right there with me. But I came
through them unscathed, in part because of my attitude of gratitude. I'm learning, Father, that keeping
my thoughts elevated is so helpful. Even when my
feet are trudging through a muddy path, I can remain
unshaken. So I'll continue to worship You even when
I'm going through rough seasons. I won't forget how
You've brought me through in the past. I'll remain
unshaken with Your help. And I will continue to offer
a sacrifice of praise even in the middle of the storm. I
praise You! Amen.

BE THE CHANGE
Honor a veteran.

Where Your Treasure Is

"Where your treasure is,
there your heart will be also."
MATTHEW 6:21 NIV

When I look back over my life, I realize that I've often placed my affections on the wrong things, Lord. Money. Cars. Houses. Jewelry. Jobs. Relationships. These things have been my treasure. The older I get though, the more I realize that You're the only treasure I need, Father. You are my all. When I put You in Your rightful place, everything else comes into alignment. I want to keep You at the center, Father. Whenever I start to lose focus and shift my attention to things instead of You, give me a little nudge. Where my treasure is, there my heart will be. May I never forget! Amen.

BE THE CHANGE
Focus on your true treasure—Jesus.

Never Ceasing

I do not cease to give thanks for you,
remembering you in my prayers.
EPHESIANS 1:16 ESV

Sometimes I struggle with consistency, Lord. I'm up one minute and down the next. I praise You with abandon one day then moan and groan the day after. That's why I'm happy for this reminder from Your Word that You want me to remain consistent in my thanks to You. May I never stop even on the hard days. My praise will accomplish even more when it's spoken through the filter of pain. So today I say, "Praise the Lord! Thanks for all You've done, all You're doing, and all You have yet to do." I really am grateful, Lord, even when I don't take the time to say it. But how powerful to utter those words aloud. I will never cease to praise You, Father. Amen.

BE THE CHANGE
Write a letter of appreciation to God
for what He has done for you.

Making Him Known

*Oh give thanks to the LORD; call upon his name;
make known his deeds among the peoples!*
PSALM 105:1 ESV

You've given me a special task, Lord: to share my
praise, my thanks, my joy with all people. It's as if
You've given me my very own microphone to carry,
one that can impact lives. But first, of course, I have
to speak up. I have to make You known. That time you
healed me when I was sick? I made You known. That
time You came to my rescue when I was going through
a rough patch with finances? I made You known. That
time I felt completely overwhelmed and wondered
why I should even get out of bed? You swept in and
restored my joy, and I shared the story with everyone
who would listen. I love to make You known, Father.
Thanks for every opportunity. Amen.

BE THE CHANGE
Think of creative ways to make Him known today.

Immeasurably More

*To him who is able to do immeasurably more than all we ask
or imagine, according to his power that is at work within us,
to him be glory in the church and in Christ Jesus throughout
all generations, for ever and ever! Amen.*
EPHESIANS 3:20–21 NIV

You are an "above and beyond" Father. You don't just
give Your kids what they need or what they ask for.
You give us immeasurably more. And it's all by Your
power not ours. That's such a relief! Why do You lavish
such goodness on me, Lord? To show Your glory both
in the church and to people who don't yet believe. For
generations, people will share the great things You've
done. I'm so grateful for the work You're doing in my
life. Amen.

BE THE CHANGE
*Go above and beyond. Take baked goods to a
local police station for the officers to enjoy.*

In All Circumstances

Give thanks in all circumstances;
for this is God's will for you in Christ Jesus.
1 THESSALONIANS 5:18 NIV

It's taken me a while to figure this one out, Lord. You long for me to praise You, to give thanks, even when I'm deep in the valley. I used to wonder if this was even possible. Now I know it is. There's something rather spectacular about stopping to worship and praise You when I'm in a low spot. It shifts my perspective off of my problems and onto You, the One with the answer. So, I will go on giving praise, no matter where I am in the journey. This is Your will for me—to lift up a song of thanksgiving in all circumstances. Amen.

BE THE CHANGE
Share your testimony with a
friend who may be inspired by it.

Admonishing One Another

*Let the message of Christ dwell among you richly as
you teach and admonish one another with all wisdom
through psalms, hymns, and songs from the Spirit,
singing to God with gratitude in your hearts.*
COLOSSIANS 3:16 NIV

I don't mind being admonished in this way, Lord! It
feels good to be encouraged by my fellow believers
with psalms, hymns, and spiritual songs. I love it when
friends take the time out of their busy days to let
me know how much they care about what I'm going
through. I want to be that kind of friend to others—
one who's in tune with what people are going through.
I want Your message to dwell so deeply inside of me
that my words of encouragement are laced with
heartfelt gratitude and wisdom from on high. In other
words, I want to be more like You, Lord. Help me, I
pray. Amen.

BE THE CHANGE

*Ask the Lord to point you in the direction of
someone who needs your encouragement today.*

Praise Leads the Way

*Enter his gates with thanksgiving and his courts
with praise; give thanks to him and praise his name.*
PSALM 100:4 NIV

I remember a story from the Bible, Lord, about a man
named Jehoshaphat. When he entered into battle, he
put his praise leaders on the front lines. The Levites
led the way. They praised their way into a war and the
battle was won—all because of praise. That's an amazing image! It reminds me that I need to praise my way
into life's tough situations. If I enter the valleys with
praise and thanksgiving on my lips, I'm more likely to
remain encouraged. And I know my faith is activated
by praise. Best of all, You love it when praise leads
the way! No matter what I'm facing, I'll give a mighty
shout and head to the front lines with "Praise You,
Lord!" on my lips. Amen.

BE THE CHANGE
Praise your way into the "frontline" battle you are facing.

Volunteer Locally

*"In all things I have shown you that by working hard
in this way we must help the weak and remember
the words of the Lord Jesus, how he himself said,
'It is more blessed to give than to receive.'"*
ACTS 20:35 ESV

Lord, I want to make a difference right here in my
town. There are so many local ministries and outreach
groups. Which ones should I help? Help me to choose
one this month, and perhaps another next. I can volunteer or give money, Lord. Or perhaps I should donate
food or clothing. The possibilities are endless, and the
need is great. I feel a gentle nudge from Your Word to
do what I can. You've told me to help the weak and to
remember (always) that it's more blessed to give than
to receive. That really resonates with me, Father, so
help me to put this verse into practice, I pray. Amen.

BE THE CHANGE
Host a baby shower for a local pregnancy center.

Nursing Homes

*He said to his disciples, "The harvest is plentiful, but the
laborers are few; therefore pray earnestly to the Lord
of the harvest to send out laborers into his harvest."*
MATTHEW 9:37–38 ESV

Father, my heart really goes out to those who are in
nursing homes. I want to help, but I don't always know
how. Should I invite my church choir to sing Christmas carols during the holiday season? Should I make
wreaths for the doors of their rooms? Should I visit
with a lonely patient who rarely has visitors? Should
I pray for the sick? There are any number of things I
could do. Jump-start me, I pray. May I put actions to
my thoughts. I want to be sent out to make an impact
to those who are feeling neglected, overlooked, or
distraught. Show me how to pray with them, minister
to them, and share Your love with them in fun and
creative ways. Amen.

BE THE CHANGE
Organize a senior prom at a local nursing home.

Compassion for Local Missions

*Be kind and compassionate to one another, forgiving
each other, just as in Christ God forgave you.*
EPHESIANS 4:32 NIV

Sometimes I simply forget, Lord, that there are hurting people all around me: from children at the local
cancer hospital to shut-ins who are unable to leave
their homes to parents caring for special needs kids.
Soup kitchens need cooks. Animal shelters are over-
run with pets in need of foster or forever homes. I see
organizations that help people and pets in need, but I
rarely think to volunteer or donate. Today, increase my
compassion, I pray. Give me a heart for a local ministry, and then show me how best to give. I'm getting
excited just thinking about the possibilities! Thanks for
using me, Lord. Amen.

BE THE CHANGE
Offer to read to patients at your local children's hospital.

Begin at Home

*"Repentance for the forgiveness of sins should
be proclaimed in his name to all nations,
beginning from Jerusalem."*
LUKE 24:47 ESV

From the time I was young, my heart was pricked
by photos of little children on the other side of the
globe—kids in need of food, medical care, and so on.
But as I've gotten older, Lord, I've started to understand the phrase "bloom where you're planted." There
are needs right here, right now. Sure, I want to impact
other parts of the world, but perhaps I should (as Your
Word says) begin in Jerusalem (my hometown). I want
to make a difference here, to come into full bloom
with local ministries. Then, when I've honed whatever
skills You want to develop in me, I'll hit the road and
travel to other places. So, help me out, Lord! Give me
courage to step out and energy to get the tasks done,
I pray. Amen.

BE THE CHANGE
*Offer to host a Christmas toy drive
for a local orphanage or foster home.*

Gentleness and Respect

A gentle tongue is a tree of life.
PROVERBS 15:4 ESV

Lord, I have to confess, I haven't always come across as gentle or respectful. Sometimes I plow into a situation, ready to make a difference, but I want to do things my way. I don't want to follow the protocol or wait on instructions. I'm so excited about making a difference that I end up doing more damage than good. May this never be! I want to be an asset to local ministries—one they know they can call on for help. I don't ever want to be a nuisance or in the way. Link me to the people who need me most, Lord. Then show me how to enter their realm with all of Your gentleness and respect, I pray. Amen.

BE THE CHANGE
Offer to wash dishes at a local halfway house.

To Seek and Save

"The Son of Man came to seek and to save the lost."
LUKE 19:10 NIV

Your Son came to seek and save the lost, Lord. And He didn't have to look far to find people in need of saving. Neither do I. I don't have to cross oceans or travel by plane to locate people who need to know Your saving grace. They encircle me on every side. My local community is filled with people who need You—in tangible ways and spiritually as well. Many need to come to faith in You, of course, but they also need practical things—food, shoes, socks, medicine, care, shelter, and so on. I want to be like Jesus. I want to seek and save the lost. May I be Your hands and feet, I pray. Amen.

BE THE CHANGE
Sponsor a kite-flying day with inner-city kids.

So Send I You

And we have seen and testify that the Father has sent his Son to be the Savior of the world.
1 JOHN 4:14 ESV

Father, You sent Your Son. You had an amazing commission for Him, a plan that would save mankind from an eternal fate. It's remarkable to think that He left the joy of heaven—pure perfection—to come to the earth, where He had to endure hardships, persecution, and rejection. You're sending me too. I feel those nudges. You want me to step up and step out—to reach my neighborhood, my community for You. You're giving me God-sized ideas for how to accomplish that. I'm not leaving heaven to do this, but I am leaving the comforts of home and a cozy life. I'm stepping out of my comfort zone. Yes, I'm nervous, but I completely trust You, Lord. Where You send, I will go, so point the way, I pray. Amen.

BE THE CHANGE
Keep a note of the many ways God has called you out of your comfort zone to serve Him.

Not to Condemn

*"God did not send his Son into the world to condemn the world,
but in order that the world might be saved through him."*
JOHN 3:17 ESV

So often the church is seen as judgmental, Lord. Many have chosen to evangelize in ways that come across as harsh. Most don't do it to hurt others, but there have been a few casualties along the way. That's why I'm asking You to show me how to speak the truth in love. When I come across people who are living their lives contrary to the way of the Gospel, I want to touch them with Your love, Your grace. But I also need to be true to Your Word. No compromises. Somewhere in the middle of the confusion, there's a way to reach them. You can do it, Father. Supernaturally. What I can't do in the flesh, You can certainly accomplish in the Spirit. Have Your way, I pray. Amen.

BE THE CHANGE
Volunteer at a facility that ministers to HIV/AIDS patients.

Power to Proclaim

"Be strong and courageous. Do not fear or be in dread of them, for it is the LORD your God who goes with you. He will not leave you or forsake you."
DEUTERONOMY 31:6 ESV

When I think about going to Jerusalem (places close to home), Judea (places a little farther away), Samaria (places farther still), and the uttermost parts of the earth (all across the globe), I feel overwhelmed. It's hard enough to reach out to local ministries. I wonder how I can help on a global scale. That's where Your Holy Spirit comes in. When I receive a touch from Him, I'm endued with power from on high. Something supernatural takes place. My courage is bolstered. My desires are quickened. My ability to get up and go is energized. Thank You, Father, for sending Your Holy Spirit to empower me. I could truly never do this alone. Amen.

BE THE CHANGE
Ask for the Holy Spirit to fill and empower you today.

Never Giving Up

*Let us not grow weary of doing good, for in
due season we will reap, if we do not give up.*
GALATIANS 6:9 ESV

Sometimes I think of the farmers planting their seeds,
Lord. They have to wait, wait, wait for the harvest to
come. How diligent they are. How patient. I tend to
run more on the impatient side. I pray for a miracle
and want it now. I reach out to a friend and expect an
immediate response. I put food in the microwave and
pull it out a minute later. But I'm working with Your
timetable now. Your Word promises that I will reap
a harvest in due season. I'm not sure when that will
come, but I have Your promise that it will happen if I
don't give up. So, I won't quit. I'll keep reaching out to
those in need. Use me, even if I get a little impatient,
Lord. Amen.

BE THE CHANGE
Host a "back to school" backpack drive for local children.

Foreign Missions

"Therefore go and make disciples of all nations, baptizing them in the name of the Father and of the Son and of the Holy Spirit, and teaching them to obey everything I have commanded you. And surely I am with you always, to the very end of the age."
MATTHEW 28:19–20 NIV

You gave this charge to all believers, to go into all the world. I think about Christians who lived a hundred years ago. Traveling to foreign nations usually meant waving goodbye to friends and family permanently (or at least for years at a time). What a sacrifice! When I was a child, I pondered this verse a lot. I wondered if You wanted all of us to get on planes and move to places on the other side of the globe. How fortunate we are to live in a time in history where we can communicate with people via the internet. What a game changer! Suddenly I see potential—through my blog, website, or social media page, I can impact people all across the world. My words could be a catalyst for change. I can raise funds, help missionaries, do all sorts of good things from the comfort of my home. What a blessing, Lord. Amen.

BE THE CHANGE
Host a missionary in your home.

The Ends of the Earth

"This is what the Lord has commanded us:
'I have made you a light for the Gentiles, that you
may bring salvation to the ends of the earth.'"
ACTS 13:47 NIV

How many people groups have still not heard the Gospel, Lord? I know the message is going out, but there are many who still haven't been reached. What can I do to help? Point me in the direction of missionaries who are traveling to unreached groups of people. I want to send my prayers, my finances, my help. I don't want to rest until everyone has had a chance to hear the life-changing message of the Gospel. Lead me to those who are making a difference so that I might link arms with them and bring lasting change. Most of all, show me how to pray more effectively for those who are lost and for those carrying the message. My heart is with them all, Lord. Amen.

BE THE CHANGE
Consider a short-term mission trip to a third-world country.

Preaching the Gospel

*He said to them, "Go into all the world
and preach the gospel to all creation."*
MARK 16:15 NIV

I've never considered myself a preacher, Lord. I'm
not sure I would know what to say if You put me up
in front of a congregation. But I'm learning there are
different ways to preach the Gospel. I can use my
creative gifts to reach children—singing, puppets,
drama. Or I can minister to people one-on-one by
praying with them and sharing my testimony. I can
help serve food and provide shoes, eyeglasses, and
medicine for them. You're not asking me to go to Bible
college and get my ministerial degree; You're simply
asking me to go when and where You call me. So, I
open myself up to the possibilities, Lord. Use me to
preach the Gospel in whatever way You choose. Amen.

BE THE CHANGE
*Volunteer for a ministry that reaches
out to children in a foreign country.*

Exalted Among the Nations!

"Be still, and know that I am God. I will be exalted among the nations, I will be exalted in the earth!"
PSALM 46:10 ESV

This is my prayer, Lord—to see Your Name exalted among the nations! I know there's coming a day when every knee will bow and every tongue will confess that You are Lord. I can't wait! What a day that will be, when those who are part of every language and tribe gather together to lift Your Name in praise. Every person in every country is precious to You. How Your heart must want to burst into song when You hear Your Name lifted in so many different languages. I can only imagine that glorious scene! Until then, show me how I can play a role in exalting You among the nations. I won't cease praying until everyone comes to know You, Lord. Amen.

BE THE CHANGE
Adopt (or sponsor) an international student.

If They Have Not Heard

*"Everyone who calls on the name of the Lord will be
saved." How, then, can they call on the one they
have not believed in? And how can they believe in
the one of whom they have not heard? And how can
they hear without someone preaching to them?*
ROMANS 10:13–14 NIV

How often do I say things like "Why don't they believe
what I believe?" or "Why don't they just stop living in
sin?" The truth is, many people are locked into their
lifestyles and their belief systems simply because they
haven't heard the Gospel message in a way that makes
sense to them. I could be that person to help them
make sense of it all, Lord. With Your help, I could make
a difference in the life of a person in my circle. I'm
open to the possibilities and pray that my flesh won't
get in the way. Whether it's here (nearby) or through
the internet/social media (online), I pray that I'm given
the opportunity to reach out to someone with the
Gospel message, for it is life to all who believe! May all
come to know You and be saved, Lord. Amen.

BE THE CHANGE
Offer to be a missionary's stateside liaison.

Food for Thought

*"I led them with cords of human kindness,
with ties of love. To them I was like one who lifts a
little child to the cheek, and I bent down to feed them."*
HOSEA 11:4 NIV

I have all I need and more, Lord. When I open my pantry door, there's food inside. I don't have to wonder where the next meal is coming from (though I've certainly been through seasons of lack in the past). I'm grateful for Your provision. Today I'm reminded of the many people across this planet who struggle to find food and water. I want to do something to help them. Show me how to link arms with a foreign missions organization to make a difference—to a whole village, if possible. I can rally my friends, Lord, and we can provide funds to feed people. I want to help so that none go hungry. Use me in this venture, I pray. Amen.

BE THE CHANGE
*Do an overseas food drive. Help a foreign
missionary to raise funds to feed a village.*

All the Little Children of the World

Declare his glory among the nations,
his marvelous deeds among all peoples.
1 CHRONICLES 16:24 NIV

I remember the song from childhood, Lord, about how
You love all the little children of the world. It brought
amazing images to mind—of little ones with different
skin colors dressed in colorful garb representing their
countries. I may never travel to the places where these
children live, but I can make a difference in other
ways. I can support an orphanage in China. I can help
a loving couple adopt a child from India. I can support
a child in Haiti. I can send Christmas packages to an
orphanage in Kenya. There are so many creative and
helpful ways to play a role, and I want to do my best
so that all the children of the world will come to know
Your Son. Amen.

BE THE CHANGE
Support a child overseas.

Supporting Missionaries

Behold, upon the mountains, the feet of him who brings good news, who publishes peace! Keep your feasts, O Judah; fulfill your vows, for never again shall the worthless pass through you; he is utterly cut off.
NAHUM 1:15 ESV

I don't know how they do it, Lord—how missionaries respond to the call to leave extended family behind and move to far-off places like Zambia, Turkey, or Afghanistan. I'm sure You're tugging on their heart-strings, and they are responding to the call. I would like to say I would respond as passionately, but I'm not altogether sure I would. Still, I want to help. I really do. The foreign mission field is huge, and the workers are few. So stir my heart as well, I pray. May I give generously, support with abandon, visit frequently, and do all I can to make my favorite missionary as productive as possible. Use me, Lord, I pray. Amen.

BE THE CHANGE
Support a ministry on a monthly basis.

The Gospel Proclaimed

"The gospel must first be proclaimed to all nations."
MARK 13:10 ESV

Today my heart is with all of the missionaries in countries that are opposed to the Gospel. Lord, I can't even imagine what they go through as they attempt to lead people to You—even when doing so is against the law. Guard and protect them, I pray. Open doors for them to visit with the right people, those whose hearts are ripe for the Gospel. Help their converts too. Give them peace, courage, and comfort as they start their new adventure with You in opposition to all around them. Please, God, protect Your children in these countries as they witness to others. I pray that Your Word spreads like wildfire and that the leaders of these countries will soon realize they must swing wide the gates for the Gospel. Amen.

BE THE CHANGE
Write a kind letter to a missionary who's struggling.

And Then the End Will Come

*"This gospel of the kingdom will be preached in
the whole world as a testimony to all nations,
and then the end will come."*
MATTHEW 24:14 NIV

And then the end will come. I remember, as a child,
pondering these words. I wondered if the return of
Your Son was imminent or if we still had time left.
Back then we didn't have the internet, so preaching
the Gospel around the world was more complicated.
Now we have ready access to people in nearly every
nation. We can spread movies, songs, testimonies—all
sorts of things. And people in other countries can (and
do) hear the message from across the globe. In fact,
the world has been so impacted by the Gospel that
many developing countries are now sending missionaries to us! Wow, Lord! What an amazing testimony
to the spreading of Your Word. We look forward with
much anticipation to the return of Your Son. Amen.

BE THE CHANGE
Make sure a missionary's kids have all they need.

Always Joyful

Always be joyful. Never stop praying.
1 THESSALONIANS 5:16–17 NLT

If I really want to impact my world and make a genu-
ine difference in the lives of those around me, Lord,
here's a good place to start! What if, from now on,
I responded to every person, every situation, every
hardship with joy? What if I never stopped praying?
What if I implemented thankfulness into my everyday
life, exuding gratitude for every act of service someone performed on my behalf, every blessing? Wouldn't
this be the best testimony ever, Father? I can almost
picture it now. People would pass by me and say, "I'll
have what you're having!" Joy is contagious after all.
Thanks for the reminder, Lord. Amen.

BE THE CHANGE
Live joyfully.

Joyful Noise

Let us come into his presence with thanksgiving;
let us make a joyful noise to him with songs of praise!
PSALM 95:2 ESV

I wouldn't say my singing voice is the best, Lord. Some days I limit my songs to the shower. But there are other days when I just want to sing out a song of praise to You—to make a joyful noise, no matter who's listening. I'm so glad You don't care about my pitch or my tone. You're only worried about my heart. And my heart is fully in tune, Lord; it is a beautiful instrument, pouring forth music for You. May others see my praise and grow curious. When they hear me humming, when they see the smile on my face, may they ask, "What's up with you? You seem pretty happy about something today." I can't wait to share the story of why You've brought such joy, Lord. Amen.

BE THE CHANGE
Spend at least ten minutes per day singing from your heart.

Joy Complete

*"I have told you this so that my joy may be
in you and that your joy may be complete."*
JOHN 15:11 NIV

It feels really good when my gas tank is filled to the tip-top, Lord! I have no worries that I'll end up stranded on the side of the road. No concerns that I'll have to hitch a ride with a stranger. I'm safe. Comfortable. Excited for the journey. That's what it's like when my joy is filled to the top as well. When my joy is "complete" (lacking nothing), it spills over onto people around me. What makes me so joyful? The work You've done in my heart and life, Lord! And I know that others are watching. They're wondering what I'm up to because I'm smiling more than usual. I'll tell them, Lord, when the timing is perfect. Open doors for me to spread the joy, I pray. Amen.

BE THE CHANGE
*Set an alarm and go for 24 hours
without criticizing anyone (or anything).*

Shouting for Joy

*Be glad in the LORD, and rejoice, O righteous,
and shout for joy, all you upright in heart!*
PSALM 32:11 ESV

I'm not always the most exuberant person, Lord. My worship is most often whispered or spoken softly. But there are times when I'm so full of joy, so overcome by Your goodness, that I want to offer up a shout of praise. When this happens, my inhibition goes! I'm ready to tell the whole world what You've done in my life—how You rescued me from sin and set my feet on a path I'll never regret. How You healed my broken heart and erased my bitterness. How You wiped away my loneliness and replaced it with godly friends who care. You've been so good to me, Father, and my heart can't help but praise! Now that's something to shout about! Amen.

BE THE CHANGE

*Find a quiet place and release a shout of praise to the Lord.
(Hint: your car is an excellent place to praise Him!)*

In His Joy I Go

*"The kingdom of heaven is like treasure hidden in a field.
When a man found it, he hid it again, and then in his
joy went and sold all he had and bought that field."*
MATTHEW 13:44 NIV

I love this story, Lord. A man stumbles across a
treasure in a field that doesn't belong to him. His joy
propels him to sell all he has to buy the field. Now the
treasure is his! This story resonates with me because
I feel like I found a treasure when I stumbled into my
relationship with You. I gave You all I had (my heart, my
life), and You gave me access to the treasure—not just
for now but for all eternity. What a good and generous
God You are. And how happy I am to be Your child. My
joy propels me to go and tell others what You've done
so that they can experience this life-altering joy too.
Help it to be so. Amen.

BE THE CHANGE
*Spend a few precious hours with
someone who needs a joy infusion.*

Joy Comes in the Morning

*His anger lasts only a moment, but his favor
lasts a lifetime! Weeping may last through
the night, but joy comes with the morning.*
PSALM 30:5 NLT

I'll confess, there have been joyless seasons in my life,
Lord—seasons where I thought the tears would never
end. I marveled that other people had smiles on their
faces when my eyes were always flooded with tears.
But Your Word promises me that joy comes in the
morning. Weeping doesn't last forever. Seasons of
grief will end, replaced by seasons of great joy. Your
favor lasts for a lifetime. It's not circumstantial. With
the dawn of each new day, I have an opportunity to
start fresh, to choose joy, to rise above the pain. Thank
You for the morning-born joy, Lord. It invigorates and
lifts me just when I need it. What a blessing. Amen.

BE THE CHANGE

*Bring joy to a teacher by helping to purchase
much-needed supplies for her classroom.*

Sowing Tears

Those who sow in tears
shall reap with shouts of joy!
PSALM 126:5 ESV

A farmer plants his seed in the ground knowing he will one day reap a harvest. I hadn't thought about it until I read this verse, Lord, but something similar happens in my life when I sow in tears. It's as if every tear drops to the ground, is planted, and springs forth as joy. Only You could accomplish this, Father. Only You could take pain and turn it into a celebration. Only You could remind me that it will all be worth it in the end. So, the next time the tears come (and I know they will), I will do my best to aim them at the soil so that they might reap a beautiful harvest. Thank You for this reminder, Father. Amen.

BE THE CHANGE

Write down the story of a time when you sowed
in tears but reaped in joy. Share your story on
social media so that others may be encouraged.

A Refuge of Joy

*Let all who take refuge in you be glad; let them
ever sing for joy. Spread your protection over them,
that those who love your name may rejoice in you.*
PSALM 5:11 NIV

I've been through troubled times, Lord—times that felt
as if they would never end. I can remember tucking
myself away from the crowd, trying to focus on You.
During those dark spells, You rushed over me like a
cloud, spreading Your arms and covering me from
danger. You were my refuge, Lord. My shelter. My
hiding place. I'm so grateful for Your umbrella of protection. You turned mourning into dancing. You turned
tears into laughter. You provided just what I needed
when I needed it. In short, Your presence changed
everything, and I've never been the same. I praise You,
Father! Amen.

BE THE CHANGE
*Want to bring a smile to a single mom's face?
Pay off her kids' school lunch tab.*

All Joy and Peace

To set the mind on the Spirit is life and peace.
ROMANS 8:6 ESV

I find it interesting, Lord, that joy and peace work hand in hand. When I'm fretting, I have neither. But when I put my trust in You, when I count on You to handle the things I can't, then I'm at peace. Being at peace brings my heart such joy that I can't contain it. This is especially noticeable when You've rescued me from a tough situation or brought me through an illness. And You love doing this for me, Lord. According to Your Word, You want to fill me as I trust in You so that I can overflow by the power of Your Spirit. This is an intentional move on Your part—and I know You do it because my joy has the power to change others. So fill me up, Lord! Amen.

BE THE CHANGE
Bring joy by swapping skills with an elderly neighbor.

Heaven Rejoices

"In the same way, there is more joy in heaven over one lost sinner who repents and returns to God than over ninety-nine others who are righteous and haven't strayed away!"
LUKE 15:7 NLT

What a fun revelation, Lord! Heaven throws a party when one sinner comes home to Jesus. A celebration takes place in the heavenly realms. What a party that must be! I can almost picture the angels high-fiving and the choir singing a rousing rendition of the "Hallelujah Chorus"! I'm tickled to hear there's rejoicing in heaven, because I'm already in rehearsal now. I'm learning to be both a recipient and giver of joy wherever I go. I want people to notice not because I want to draw attention to myself but to You, Lord. You are the ultimate joy giver after all. My heart overflows when I think about all You've done for me. Here's to an eternity of joy, Lord! Amen.

BE THE CHANGE
Put on a play for seniors.

Affecting Eternity

*"God so loved the world that he gave his one
and only Son, that whoever believes in him
shall not perish but have eternal life."*
JOHN 3:16 NIV

It's sobering to think that my actions could affect eternity, but I know it's true. My attitude today could sway someone either to a lifetime with You or a decision to avoid Christianity altogether. This is one reason I desire to live a holy, godly life—because I know You long for me to be a good witness, a good representation of You while I have the chance. So don't let me waste a moment, Lord! Shift my focus from myself to others, from a life of self-gain to a life of giving. Effecting change has become increasingly more important to me. Here's to spending a lifetime in heaven with the people I impact today. Amen.

BE THE CHANGE

Host a weekly prayer group in your home.

Hearing and Believing

"Truly, truly, I say to you, whoever hears my word and believes him who sent me has eternal life. He does not come into judgment, but has passed from death to life."
JOHN 5:24 ESV

In order for my friends and family to spend eternity with You, Lord, they have to be exposed to Your salvation message. Most of them know that I'm a believer, but I don't always know how to reach them. (Isn't it strange that it's harder to reach out to my family members than total strangers, Lord? Why is that?) I want to make a difference in their lives, but it's such a careful balance with those I'm closest to. Some of these folks really know how to push my buttons! But I won't give up. It's more important to me than anything, making sure those I love come to a saving relationship with You. Help me, I pray. Amen.

BE THE CHANGE

Be who you say you are, especially in front of family and friends. Make sure your actions and attitude match your faith message.

What Good Thing Must I Do?

*Just then a man came up to Jesus and asked,
"Teacher, what good thing must I do to get eternal life?"*
MATTHEW 19:16 NIV

I'm a worker bee, Lord. Of course, You already know this. You created me after all. When it comes to eternity though, my hard work will never be enough to get me through heaven's door. I think about the story of the man who asked Jesus, "What good thing must I do to get eternal life?" He was a lot like me, I guess—looking to himself for answers. Jesus gave him a lot to think about, especially when He suggested the man take his eyes off his possessions and wealth. Ouch. You're teaching me a lot through stories like this—mostly that I'm not my own savior. I am reliant on You, God, not just to open heaven's door but to get me through this life. Thank You for doing what I couldn't do for myself. I'm eternally grateful, Father. Amen.

BE THE CHANGE
*Make a list of all the things Jesus has done
for you that you could not do for yourself.*

Eternity in Your Heart

He has made everything beautiful in its time. He has also set eternity in the human heart; yet no one can fathom what God has done from beginning to end.
ECCLESIASTES 3:11 NIV

You put it there, Lord. You set the desire to live forever in my heart. It was always Your desire to have us with You for all eternity. Long before Adam and Eve made a sinful choice in the garden, You had this plan in motion—Your kids would be with You not just in this lifetime but also the one to come. Sin tried to interrupt this plan, but Your Son came to remedy that. For those of us who place our trust in You, eternity is very real. We can taste it, smell it, and sense it coming. I can't fathom the amazing things that await me in heaven, but I'm guessing it's all going to be pretty remarkable. You've been working on eternity for, well, an eternity. Thank You. Amen.

BE THE CHANGE
*Develop an eternal perspective.
Always keep heaven in mind.*

This Is Eternal Life

"This is eternal life: that they know you, the only true God, and Jesus Christ, whom you have sent."
JOHN 17:3 NIV

There is no eternal life without You, God. No one enters heaven's gates without coming to a saving relationship with Your Son. That's why it's so important that I let people know. It's not enough to just assume people are ready for heaven—I have to know for sure. Jesus is eternal life. And it's Jesus I have to share—with my family, my friends, my coworkers, my neighbors. Show me how to go about this, I pray. I don't want to put up any walls or cause division. Make my words grace-filled so that I may be most effective. Give me opportunities to share what You've done in my life. I will proclaim Your goodness, Lord, and watch You move. Amen.

BE THE CHANGE
Offer to help your neighbor with a cumbersome task.

Eternal Praise

The fear of the LORD is the beginning of wisdom;
all who follow his precepts have good understanding.
To him belongs eternal praise.
PSALM 111:10 NIV

I love worshipping You, Father, whether it's through song, prayer, Bible reading, or proclaiming Your Name. When I think about what worship services are going to be like in heaven, I get so excited. Sometimes I like to think about what the music will sound like. Is Mozart already composing new melodies? Are some of the world's greatest opera singers warming up their voices in preparation? What will it be like to have the finest musicians and the most amazing singers all together in one place, leading us out in heavenly chorus? The mind reels, Father. I can hardly wait to see (and hear) it all for myself. Amen.

BE THE CHANGE
Invite your neighbor to church.

Eternal Perspective

Since we believe that Jesus died and rose again,
even so, through Jesus, God will bring with
him those who have fallen asleep.
1 THESSALONIANS 4:14 ESV

It's hard to think about death sometimes, Lord. I get
so focused on the person I've lost, the one who is no
longer with me, that I forget the glory being experienced. I want my loved ones to come back for one
last visit, but they wouldn't trade heaven for anything!
From the moment they crossed from death to life,
all memories of the earth became distant. So, I won't
wish them back. I'll release them to You. Instead of
focusing on how I feel, help me to shift my thoughts.
Give me glimpses of what they are doing in heaven.
Singing? Worshipping? Getting reacquainted with
people they haven't seen in years? Oh, I can hardly
imagine, Lord, but I'm sure it's glorious. Thank You for
an eternal perspective! Amen.

BE THE CHANGE
Make a list of all the people you can't wait to see in heaven.

The Gift of God

*The wages of sin is death, but the gift of
God is eternal life in Christ Jesus our Lord.*
ROMANS 6:23 NIV

Salvation is a free gift, one that I'm eternally thankful
for, Lord. It cost me nothing (except my heart), but
it cost Your Son everything. You've asked that I share
this gift with others—and I'm trying! Sometimes, in the
moment, I freeze up. I can't think of what to say. I
haven't memorized the verses or worked up the courage to speak up. That's where You come in. Your Holy
Spirit energizes me, reminds me of all I've received
in my own life, and gives me the oomph that I need
to share that story with others. Before long, they're
ready to receive that free gift too. Salvation truly is
the gift that keeps on giving. I praise You! Amen.

BE THE CHANGE
*Memorize the Romans Road (the verses in
Romans that speak of how to be saved).*

In My Father's House

*"In my Father's house are many rooms. If it were not so,
would I have told you that I go to prepare a place for you?
And if I go and prepare a place for you, I will come again
and will take you to myself, that where I am you may be also."*
JOHN 14:2–3 ESV

Oh how I love this scripture, Lord! It personalizes
heaven and makes me feel like I already belong there.
Jesus has already gone to prepare a place for me. This
makes my heart so happy. I feel like a kid again, with
my daddy painting my room a lovely shade of pink
and my mama sewing curtains. I'm loved. I'm accepted.
I have a place prepared just for me, with all the things
I love. You're going to personally escort me to this
home, Lord. That's the biggest blessing of all. You'll be
with me every step of the way, welcoming me through
the doorway, arms extended, tears of joy in Your eyes.
I can't wait to spend eternity with You, Lord. Amen.

BE THE CHANGE

*Read everything the Bible has to say about heaven so
that you can share what you've learned with others.*

From Eternity to Eternity

"From eternity to eternity I am God. No one can snatch anyone out of my hand. No one can undo what I have done."
ISAIAH 43:13 NLT

Father, sometimes I like to think about what You were doing before You ever created mankind. I try to imagine it all—before stars, planets, rivers, and mountains. Before animals, plants, or sneaky snakes in the garden. Before morning, noon, and night. If I'm being totally honest, it's too much for my finite mind to comprehend. Your concept of time is vastly different from my own. If I believe in eternity (and I do) then I have to believe that there was no beginning and there will be no end. You always were—and You always will be. You were present before, You are present now, and You will be present for all eternity. And, best of all, You loved me then, You love me now, and You'll go on loving me forever. Amen.

BE THE CHANGE
*Begin to see everyone you know
through the filter of eternity.*

Scripture Index

OLD TESTAMENT

NEW TESTAMENT

KIDS CAN CHANGE THE WORLD TOO WITH. . .

180 Prayers to Change the World for Kids

This fantastic prayer book for the kids in your life
will put the amazing power of prayer into perspective
as they pray for their friends, their families, their
neighborhoods, their schools, their cities, their
country, and beyond. Kids ages 8 to 12 will be
guided to pray for positive change in the world as
they encounter the many ways they can make an
impact through their conversations with God.

Paperback / 978-1-64352-016-2 / $4.99